Fee-Based Services in Library and Information Centres

Second Edition

(formerly entitled 'Making a charge for library
and information services', Aslib, 1994)

Sylvia P Webb

and

Jules Winterton

Fee-Based Services in Library and Information Centres

Second Edition

(formerly entitled 'Making a charge for library and information services', Aslib, 1994)

Sylvia P Webb
and
Jules Winterton

Routledge
Taylor & Francis Group
NEW YORK AND LONDON

Second Edition

© Sylvia P Webb and Jules Winterton 2003

First published 2003 by Europa Publications Limited

This edition published 2013 by Routledge

2 Park Square, Milton Park, Abingdon, Oxon OX14 4RN
711 Third Avenue, New York, NY 10017

Routledge is an imprint of the Taylor & Francis group an informa busin

ISBN 978-0-851-42475-0

Contents

About the authors

Sylvia Webb, founding editor of the Know How series, is a well-known consultant, author and lecturer in the information management field. Her first book *Creating an Information Service*, now in its third edition, has sold in over 40 countries. She has experience of working in both the public and private sectors, from public libraries to national and international organisations. She has also been a lecturer at Ashridge Management College, specialising in management and inter-personal skills, which led to her second book, *Personal Development in Information Work.* Since then she has written several titles for the Know How series, and numerous articles. She has served on a number of government advisory bodies, has been regularly involved in professional activities and was a Vice-President of the former Institute of Information Scientists. (The Library Association and the Institute of Information Scientists merged in April 2002 to become the Chartered Institute of Library and Information Professionals.)

Jules Winterton is the Librarian and Deputy Director of the Institute of Advanced Legal Studies (IALS), University of London. He is the Vice-President of the International Association of Law Libraries and former Chair of the British and Irish Association of Law Librarians. He is responsible for a fee-based information service for the legal profession operated by the IALS. He has lectured and written on legal bibliography, legal research and library management and conducts regular workshops on financial planning for information services. He has acted as a consultant to law libraries in the United Kingdom and overseas. His publications include the second edition of *Information Sources in Law* (Winterton and Moys, 1997).

Acknowledgements

Thanks are due to the organisations that have shared their experiences and agreed to the use of these as examples and case studies in this publication. We would like to thank in particular those individuals who so willingly provided information or prepared case material, namely: Pamela Bater and Anna Burmajster of the Institute of Directors; Alice Hamilton, former Legal Information Services Manager at the Institute of Advanced Legal Studies; Kate Hodgson, Head of Knowledge and Information Management at CMS Cameron McKenna; Margaret Pratt, Manager of MONINFO at Monash University; Susana Vasquez, Manager of IFS Information Service and Sarah Watts, Manager, BRIS, both at the Institute of Financial Services; and Susan Watt, Manager of the London Business School Information Service.

Chapter 1

Why charge?

Introduction

The aim of this guide is to set out the key considerations for decision-makers involved in putting into practice ideas for a priced service, as part of overall library and information service (LIS) provision. Whether you are operating in the public or private sector, the decisions required about introducing a service for which a charge is to be made, and the processes involved, are likely to be very similar, even if organizational objectives are different. Decisions will relate to assessing and identifying the market, long- and short-term planning, costing and pricing, staffing and delivery, and general resources. The user groups may vary, as will the specifics of each service, but efficient management and planning will be common to all.

The process will involve regular user consultation and management review, as well as active marketing and promotion. Above all it will need to be viewed by top management as a valuable and integral part of a co-ordinated organisational policy. Four case studies describing real-life approaches to various aspects of developing and operating a priced service are provided in chapter 8. These illustrate the ways in which two academic libraries, a professional body, and a firm of solicitors have handled the introduction and development of charging for library and information services.

Fee or free

The notion of making a charge to users of library and information services is not new even in the context of free public library services. As far back as the 1950s and 1960s there was debate about the subject in the professional press. However, in those early years the focus was largely on charging fines for overdue books, charging a minimal sum to cover postage for book reservations and making a charge for use to non-residents in the case of public libraries. University libraries considered similar aspects of their services as appropriate for such charges, with non-affiliated persons rather than non-residents being subject to charges for use. Additional services such as the loan of recorded music and of video recordings in public libraries were also considered suitable for charges and needed to cover their costs if existing services were not to suffer.

A change of approach became apparent from the 1970s onwards. Technology, particularly in making available online services, and the rapid take-up of these services, alerted LIS managers not only to the potential for improving service and providing access to a far wider range of source material than before, but also to the very real possibility of a rapid escalation of costs. Unlike the one-off purchase price associated with buying a reference book, or the annual subscription to a journal, both allowing subsequent unlimited use at no extra cost, the online service usually raised a charge each time it was used. There were a few databases that offered a fixed annual subscription rate, but these rates were often quite high unless considerable use was made of them. There were also high costs for telecommunications, technical infrastructure and support, which led to a higher level of overheads. Competition between electronic information providers and the introduction of generic web-based delivery have moderated some of these increases.

However, the possibilities and costs of providing new services or existing services in new formats, for example in recent years the provision of Internet access in public libraries, raise the same issues.

By the 1980s small-scale cost recovery was not the sole reason for making a charge in the LIS environment. Information was being promoted as a valuable commodity which was essential to decision-making and part of competitor intelligence gathering. For this reason information was seen as something on which a price should be put with the potential for making a profit. Charges could be made to internal and external clients of the organisation, in the latter case offering an additional range of services. The early "fee or free" arguments are well set out by practitioners in "Fees for library service" (1986), a special issue of the journal *Collection Building*. Charging still remains a controversial issue in some quarters but it is not likely to go away. Coffman (1999), as director of a fee-based information service at the County of Los Angeles Public Library, addresses the ongoing "fee or free" debate and provides a robust defence of the value of such services.

Attitudes within the LIS profession have moved on, and in 2003 the notion of charging for some services is more widely accepted than it was in the 1980s. While access to a range of publicly provided core library and information services is still regarded as being a key contributor to culture and education, and therefore must continue to be made freely available to society at large, it is no longer regarded as unethical or unacceptable by most LIS practitioners to introduce charges for certain specialist services. This may be a result of closer scrutiny of costs and the changing demands on service provision, or part of other changes in corporate policy. It could be caused by the introduction or wider use of internal charging, with greater emphasis on transparency, which gives a more precise picture of the use made of various internal functions. Another possible cause is the increasingly narrow identification of funding streams with their target constituencies which offers less discretion in allowing others to benefit from the services without contributing to the funding.

Charging of any kind can lead to a possible conflict of interest in terms of achieving overall objectives, as Will (2000) demonstrates. He outlines the difficulties which can be experienced in operating a widely available free public service (in this case by a government-funded scientific research institution) once charges are introduced. Most fee-based information services operate within the wider context of their parent organisation, often within a broader library and information service that may not have the same overall commercial imperative. It is essential to make clear decisions in advance about the relationship and how the missions of the two operations complement each other. There is a possibility that conflicts may arise if priorities cannot be determined, particularly if services draw on shared resources, whether they are staff resources, building space, technical or administrative infrastructure, or a physical collection of information materials. For example, a service based on an existing library may tend to influence collection development policies to obtain material that is of interest to fee-paying clients but of less interest to the readers for whom the library is primarily funded. A fee-based information service may provide different levels of service such as a faster response; if turnover increases, this may draw staff away from services to the primary constituency of the library. It is important that there is no hidden resource subsidy of the fee-based service from the parent organisation as this will cause conflict and resentment and will tend to undermine the stability of both services.

Management and planning implications

Organisations outside the public domain, chiefly commercial and industrial companies, have long seen the LIS function as one which needs to operate as any other department, being accountable and able to justify its expenditure, and increasingly to generate income. This approach is now viewed as one which is transferable across the public/private divide. Charging is seen as playing an important role in resource planning by clarifying need and usage. Even if cash does not change hands, as in the case of internal charging, the activity of assessing and recording the amount of staff time spent, the cost of obtaining and supplying information, and the amount of use by different organisational functions, helps present a much clearer picture of supply and demand.

Management skills have become as important to the LIS manager as to the Head of Marketing, and so has recognition of the vital role played by information services in an organisation. The argument goes something like this: "Information has a value but only if it is known about and readily available. The information expert holds the key and thus should also be valued." As the "fee or free" debate got under way, this approach seemed to set in motion a campaign (if not a co-ordinated one) which still continues: to raise the profile of those individuals providing library and information services. However, recognition does not just happen; users and potential users of a service need to be made aware of the range of knowledge and skills to which they have access, as well as the information. So in came terms like "value-added services" linking personal skills to the value of information provided, producing an enhanced information end-product, rather than just pointing an enquirer towards

5

the source in which an answer might be found.

Intermediaries could now be seen in several different ways: advising the enquirer on appropriate sources, whether printed or electronic; assisting and training enquirers in the use of such sources; or discovering and packaging information in such a way that it did not require the enquirer to do further research, but allowed immediate use of the information as provided. In addition, recognition alongside other professions started to be seen as desirable; if the time of lawyers and accountants can have a market value put on it and be quantified in terms of "chargeable time", why not that of LIS professionals, especially those operating within legal, accounting or other professional firms? This point is emphasized in the CMS Cameron McKenna case study in chapter 8.

Another reason put forward for making a charge is that of coming into line with commercial providers of information. In this case the question is not "Why charge?" but rather "Why not charge?" If the local business community needs information for business development purposes but companies choose not to set up in-house services, then there is a potential market for an external fee-based service. This can be provided by any local centre with the appropriate resources and expertise, whether it is a public library, a business school, a company, or some other sort of institution.

A major influence on LIS operators across the public and private sectors, encouraging them to consider charging as an option, has been the changing economic climate, and in particular changes in central and local government funding. Budget cuts, "value for money" policies, calls for increased efficiency and effectiveness, as well as for more accountability and scrutiny of the use of resources, have all led LIS managers to rethink their approach to budgeting and planning.

Another key factor in the development of fee-based services has been technology: software to assist in the management planning process, additional electronic or telecommunications-based products from which to offer new services such as real-time financial information, digital imaging, and of course the Internet. Web pages and communication by email have alerted not only internal users, but also potential external enquirers to information services which they might not otherwise have discovered. LIS managers across the sectors have commented on the increase in the number and range of internal and external enquiries, which they see as resulting directly from their web site. While it is good to be recognized as a centre of excellence, it can also lead to unsolicited enquiries which you may not be able to answer, either because they are outside your subject area or because they are outside your remit as a largely internal provider. In this case you will need to be aware of appropriate providers to whom you can refer the enquirer. This is how the Information Service of the Institute of Directors, which does not charge members separately for its services, operates.

The Institute of Directors offers its membership direct access to its Business Information Service from anywhere in the world. It is free of charge and for members only. It offers to handle 25 enquiries per member per year and to spend professional research time of up to 30 minutes per enquiry. It also guarantees that information will be supplied within 24 hours. A charge will only be passed on for any external services used and only with prior agreement of the member making the enquiry. In addition to information, the Institute offers several advisory services, although its brochure cautions that "the service offers brief advice, not lengthy consultancy".

New services can provide a useful means by which to introduce the notion of charging. It is not a good idea to introduce charges randomly for existing and unchanged services which have previously been free at the point of delivery. No one will be keen to pay for something that they might be able to get elsewhere without being charged. Careful consideration should be given if the effect of introducing charging is to withdraw public funding from an existing public service. We need to remember that the user is already likely to be making some form of financial contribution to a number of services that appear to be "free", e.g. the taxpayer for public and academic libraries, and clients and members in the case of other organisations. It is important to present the concept of charging in a positive and acceptable way. Those being asked to pay should understand the justification for the charge. This needs to be more than the notion that management has woken up to the fact that it has always cost money to provide the service, but this just did not feature in the plan - if there was one. Making a charge for new or expanded services, perhaps gradually phasing out or upgrading old services, is all part of having a strategy.

Before introducing charges for any service it is essential to consider where the service sits within your long-term objectives and priorities and establish that:

- there is a need for the service
- there is a willingness to pay
- you have the appropriate resources and skills to take it forward.

So before proceeding any further, you will need to address these issues by reviewing resources and researching the market. Only then will you be able to start constructing a plan which is likely to be viable.

Chapter 2

Getting started

Your initial considerations will focus on the following key points:

- what you can offer
- why you are charging
- what resources you will need.

These will have to be set against what is already available in the marketplace and what your users perceive as being their requirements. Before you can set about testing the market a lot of careful planning will need to be done. It is best to treat this whole exercise as a project and to plan it as a series of stages, each of which cannot be started before the preceding one has been satisfactorily concluded. This will be necessary whether the charging is to internal or external clients.

Brainstorming

One way of getting started is to have an initial brainstorming session among all the staff likely to be involved, setting out the random thoughts for consideration as they are mentioned, possibly using the "mind map" or "brain dump" approach, as described below. Although spontaneous at the time that it is in progress, brainstorming requires participants to understand fully the session's purpose and know how it works as an activity. They should be given the problem or situation to be addressed a day or so in advance. The idea is to generate as many ideas as possible, so allow enough time for this, and for participants not to feel inhibited about putting forward unconventional ideas. The atmosphere must encourage contributions of all kinds. What is sought is a solution, a way forward, and this may produce an unexpected but effective new direction.

Mind maps

This is a simple technique whereby you set out the topic that you want to develop, usually written in a circle or square, in the centre of the flipchart page. As people offer ideas you add these on a series of lines coming out from the centre. Related ideas can be roughly grouped together as they occur (see Figure 2.1).

You will undoubtedly have a number of other considerations to add to those shown in the example. Mind maps do not have to be in this format - some people find the column approach works better, where a broad heading for each new aspect raised starts a new column, and related ideas are put into the relevant column providing an initial rough sorting. Both methods work best if there is a large flipchart and enough wall space to display sheets side by side around the room. This allows consideration of all the ideas at the same time, which in turn will trigger additional thoughts. It is important that all staff understand the justification for the new arrangements - apart from anything else, they are likely to have to explain these to the users. Involving all staff in this first stage will not only bring about understanding and generate a wide range of possible opportunities and issues for consideration, but also raise interest, enthusiasm and support among staff to take the project forward.

It is also important at this stage to appoint a project leader who will co-ordinate activities and act as point of reference as the project develops. The leader may be the LIS manager, or could be someone who has been

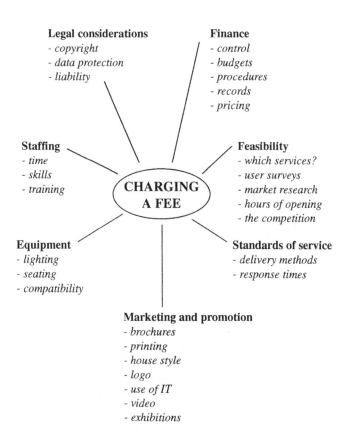

Legal considerations
- *copyright*
- *data protection*
- *liability*

Finance
- *control*
- *budgets*
- *procedures*
- *records*
- *pricing*

Staffing
- *time*
- *skills*
- *training*

CHARGING
A FEE

Feasibility
- *which services?*
- *user surveys*
- *market research*
- *hours of opening*
- *the competition*

Equipment
- *lighting*
- *seating*
- *compatibility*

Standards of service
- *delivery methods*
- *response times*

Marketing and promotion
- *brochures*
- *printing*
- *house style*
- *logo*
- *use of IT*
- *video*
- *exhibitions*

Figure 2.1: Example of a "mind-map" as
developed in a brainstorming session

appointed specifically to develop and run the fee-based service as it comes into operation.

At the end of the initial brainstorming, you will need to sieve the ideas generated, discard inappropriate ones and re-group those that remain for further consideration. After a final shake-up, the shape of the project should emerge as a series of activities to be pursued within a stated timetable. These activities can then be allocated to appropriate members of staff, where necessary bringing in outside specialist help, for example legal, technical or financial advice.

Project team meetings will need to be set up for regular progress reviews. They are particularly important, not just as a means of recording and co-ordinating progress, but also as a communications vehicle through which all participants are kept in touch with the project as a whole. The meetings will also act as a forum in which problems can be raised and solutions sought. They will help ensure steady progress and adherence to the timetable preventing bottlenecks and delays. They will also assist in the teambuilding and teamworking necessary to a successful project.

Staff training needs

A range of staff training needs will become apparent. Ways of addressing these must be built into the project plan. Various skills and knowledge will be required if the new service is to be a long-term success. Managers will require technical knowledge, people management skills, some expertise in marketing and distribution and other commercial skills, knowledge of legal issues and strategic planning ability. Attitudes and understanding are equally important. For example, if you are planning a business information service, those dealing with the users of that service will need not only to understand the terminology and language of business, and to be aware of new issues and developments in a rapidly moving field, but also to understand the business culture and the way in which it operates. The significance of commercial skills in today's LIS environment is constantly mentioned at conferences and courses. These skills are needed in a variety of activities and tasks, such as promotion of the service and the ability to interact effectively with users. Diplomacy and assertiveness will be needed in order to present developments in the context of a clear overall organisational rationale, rather than merely putting a case forward from a narrow departmental viewpoint.

Training to put relevant skills into place will enable those involved to respond to demands in the most appropriate and efficient way. When users are charged for a service they tend to be more alert to, and critical of, any perceived failings. The areas for training, whether knowledge- or skills-based, and the methods to be used will need to be considered in the light of the specific service offered and the previous experience and training of the individual member of staff. Some may need just a refresher course in certain areas, such as an update on sources, others will need more detailed training.

The initial planning of the service will have to take into account the needs of all the staff involved, whether they are assigned full-time to the fee-based service, or participate only occasionally, on a rota basis, or as relief staff to cover holidays or sickness.

Interpersonal skills, work management including time management, and the ability to assign priorities will play key parts in any venture. Both external and internal training activities are likely to be used. Staff already familiar with, and experienced in the field may carry out some of the training. Allowance will need to be made for training costs and time in any preliminary costing exercise and in longer-term budgeting. Staff, skills and team-work underpin the success of the Business Research and Information Service (BRIS), as noted in the case study in chapter 8, which also illustrates the importance of consultation in developing a pricing strategy.

Chapter 3

Market research

At this stage you will need to carry out and co-ordinate your market research. You have to establish what you want to sell as "products"; the resources required to deliver them efficiently and effectively; and who else is operating in the field. If you are planning to introduce charged services aimed at external clients, this research will confirm whether or not there really is a market. If you are going to start passing on costs to internal clients, you will need to review what is currently on offer and how this relates to users' perceived future needs. Perhaps you are doing both; if so your internal clients will have to be reassured that their information provision will not suffer as a result of the additional demands that will be made on the overall service. You might also want to involve your internal clients in promoting the external service to their business and professional contacts.

Information audit

Research that can be carried out internally will concern resources - both staff and information - and internal clients, their views and use of the existing service, and their anticipated future information needs. Any review of LIS information resources should be carried out as part of an overall organisational information audit. Only by carrying out such a review will you be able to assess the total information resource available to users and to you in planning the future direction of the LIS. Like any other audit this will involve a methodical and detailed examination of assets, in this case information assets held throughout the organisation, not just within the LIS. This is important in terms of the overall resource on which you can draw; it also has financial implications, for instance, whether or not to duplicate sources held and used as working tools in other departments. Subject expertise should also be considered as a valuable part of the total information resource. Methods of carrying out an information audit are described by Steve Thornton in Scammell (2001, 128-143). The information audit (what you *have*) will need to be followed by an information needs analysis (what you *need*). This is discussed a little later under internal and external client surveys.

Apart from reviewing information resources, you will also need to consider financial and staff resources which support the use of information. Go back through your budgets and perhaps have a discussion with the finance manager who may be able to put the figures into perspective and offer other advice, for example on rates for staff time, on financial controls and on pricing policy. Further discussions will probably be necessary at a later stage on the related administrative procedures and recording systems which you will want to put into place (see the CMS Cameron McKenna case study in chapter 8). In the context of a staff resource review, the sort of information that you will want to draw together will relate to salaries and other costs of employment, times of availability, levels of skills and ability, experience and prior training. All this information will help in determining the potential contribution that each person could make to any new or changed service and indicate the amount and type of additional training that each may need. In terms of overall planning it will also provide an indication of other possible staffing requirements for specific services.

The competition

The internal research that you have carried out in respect of resources and expertise will give you a platform from which to assess their strengths or limitations as a basis for offering an external service. However, you will also need to judge them by considering the resource base on which competing external services draw. Your market may be a local one based on geographical considerations of ease of access and familiarity with that part of the community that you are targeting. On the other hand you may be aiming at a niche market with a particular subject requirement in which you are able to offer specialist skills and information sources. In order to be able to assess your potential market, you will need to seek answers to the following questions:

- Who is offering the same type of product?
- What charges do they make?
- What methods of delivery do they offer?
- Where are they located?
- What is their target catchment area?
- What resources and expertise do they have and use?
- How do they promote their services?
- Who are their clients?

Providers of services of any kind need clients and will want to encourage and impress new ones. Don't underestimate the value of a simple telephone enquiry made by you to providers about their services. This will generate useful initial information. It will also provide a valuable insight into the degree of understanding of your stated need, the speed of response and general style of a service with which you might be competing. Providers' resources are likely to be described in brochures or other promotional material that they publish, as well as on their websites, of which you should make a thorough search. Resources listed on websites will be key features of providers' services, often establishing their authority and experience in the field. Entries in directories such as *Where to Buy Business Information* (Broadhurst and Brown, 1999), along with evaluative articles in journals, will help you to discover further details about providers. You should note in particular prices and methods of delivery, things which could give any provider a competitive edge. Try to see the service in action through a personal visit if the service centre is open to clients. Arrange to have demonstrations of any electronic services; talk to representatives at exhibitions and conferences. Feedback from colleagues in other organisations who may be past or present users of a provider will be invaluable. You may decide actually to test the service by using it yourself for a limited period; see the one-off expenditure as a market research cost that could save you a lot of time and effort in your planning, as well as leading to a better-defined product profile and more clearly identified potential client base for your own service.

During the course of your investigations you may discover providers who offer similar but not identical services to your own. They may perhaps cover a different but related subject field or target a different sector or geographical area. Even at the outset and certainly as a service becomes established, you should consider the benefits of forming strategic alliances. These may simply enable you to refer clients whose requests you cannot meet to alliance partners or may lead to the development of more fundamental partnerships, with many potential advantages.

User consultation and input

Whichever type of charging you are considering, internal or external, you will need to consult current and potential users to help you to understand their information needs and the potential demand for your services. The process of surveying internal and external clients is discussed below and Jan Sykes outlines the process of information needs assessment in Scammell (2001, 111-127).

Before you actively investigate the needs of current and potential users it is essential that you have a clear picture in your own mind of recorded usage and demand to date. This can be assessed from an analysis of enquiries and service requests, looking at the numbers and frequency, the complexity and degree of detail required, the subject areas covered, the sources used, costs involved, time constraints and deadlines to be met, and the degree of user satisfaction with the outcome if this has been expressed or measured in any way. This presupposes detailed recording of such information, which most LIS managers with an enquiry-centred service would normally keep as a key component of overall management planning.

In the context of this guide, internal clients or users are defined as those who are employed by the same organisation within which the LIS operates. External clients will therefore be those who are not employees but wish to make use of a particular information resource in the LIS to which they do not have access in their own organisation. This may be because their own employers do business with the parent organisation of the LIS, or because they know the LIS to be a centre of excellence, or because the LIS operates as a commercial service to external clients, such as that offered by the London Business School Library and its separate Information

Service (see Appendix for contact details). Then there are those external clients who have another reason: an affiliation such as that of membership of a professional association, which may entitle them to use of the library and information services, some without any charge over and above the membership fee, such as the Institute of Directors mentioned earlier (see Appendix for contact details), while other membership bodies may charge only for specified services.

In the case of a public library, although almost all users could be said to be external, there will also be those who may not live in the area, but whose place of work is nearby. Therefore, for personal convenience, or because that branch of the public library has a comprehensive specialist collection in a field of interest, these people may wish to make regular use of it. Fee-based information services specifically aimed at business are offered by numerous public libraries, institutions, chambers of commerce and commercial organisations, many of which are listed in *Where to Buy Business Information* (Broadhurst and Brown, 1999).

Internal client surveys

User surveys will need to be carefully structured to ensure that they can be carried out as efficiently as possible, without taking too much of the user's time. The most effective way is likely to be through the face-to-face interview, but this requires planning. First, draw up a questionnaire or detailed checklist that will provide the structure for the interview. Set a time limit - people are much more willing to talk to you if there is a stated end-time. Make appointments in advance, having already circulated a note (by paper or email) about the purpose of the interviews. Save clients' and potential clients' time by finding out beforehand as much as you can about their areas of responsibility and therefore likely information needs, for instance by talking to those who work with them, or by looking through internal documents such as house journals and departmental reports. The checklist or questionnaire will assist you in covering all the points on which you need information, but do allow time for other issues to be raised that may provide useful additional food for thought; see Webb (1996) for further discussion of the information needs analysis. If face-to-face interviews are not possible then a questionnaire can be circulated in paper or email format. Suggest an early return date on the form itself so that you can move on to the analysis as soon as possible. Contributors to such activities often appreciate some sort of feedback on the outcome of the survey, however brief, so do give them an indication of what form this may take, for instance a short memorandum, or a note by email or on a bulletin board. Your experience of generating responses by various means will determine which is likely to be most effective.

If you introduce charging internally, you will be working with a clearly identifiable and constant client base. Users will also be colleagues familiar with the organisational climate, working to the same overall objectives, often using the same standard procedures. This last point is important in that there may already be appropriate administrative tools and techniques in place which you can, or must, use. You will have easier access to, and probably more regular contact with, internal users than you might in a service aimed at a more broadly based and random user group. Consultation should therefore be more straightforward, but the rules of good communication still apply. Don't forget, you are hoping to attract those who may not at present use or support the internal service, even though they could benefit from it. There will also be those who see an internal service as one which should satisfy all their information needs, whether or not these are directly work-related. These clients might see charging and the need for recording each work project to which an information request relates as a threat, an intrusion or an erosion of perceived "rights".

External client surveys

External clients will fall into two main categories:

- regular users - possibly already clients of your organisation for other services, e.g. in the case of an accounting firm

- occasional (or possibly one-off) users - providing less opportunity for regular consultation and feedback.

The first category will represent users whom you probably know through their regular use, making contact easier. The second category could include those using other services of your organisation but only occasionally using the LIS. This category would also be likely to apply to those using the services run by a public library or by other external institutions of which they are members. Possible ways of surveying external clients include the questionnaire, either used as the basis for face-to-face interviews at the library where the service will be based, or as part of selective mailing by post or email to targeted groups such as local businesses or members of professional associations. You could also either refer to the survey with contact details on your website or put up the questionnaire in full. Of course you will be able to target a wide audience via your website. However, as you will have observed from looking at those of other organisations, web pages vary considerably in their ease and possible speed of use, as well as their visual attractiveness. If you are seeking feedback within a given time frame, make sure that this particular item is prominently displayed, shows your cut-off date, and is in a form that encourages response. The new service could also be outlined and response sought in any composite client brochures describing the full range of organisational services. Whatever your method of communication, if it might be seen as marketing your services, do check on any legal considerations concerning unsolicited mailings. In the United Kingdom you could usefully start by checking with the Direct Marketing Association (see Appendix for contact details).

Other ways of eliciting response would be by reproducing the questionnaire in local newspapers or specialist journals, or publishing a piece asking for responses. Leaflets with a tear-off response slip and notices displayed in the LIS, or handed out to users, could also help in the process. Whatever method you choose, you must ensure that material is well prepared and presented so that it will receive attention and promote the planned service in an appropriate way. You will also need to decide on the number and type of users to survey in order to provide a valid sample.

Willingness to pay

Whether external or internal, information clients are those who need access to one or more specialist collections in the form of libraries or information centres operated by staff whom they can trust to understand and meet their information needs comprehensively, accurately and usually quickly. The value of having the information may exceed any concerns the user might have about the price.

Egholm and Jochumsen (2000) report on an investigation into user attitudes towards fee-based services in the public library sector. In Aarhus, Denmark's second largest city, 4,500 users responded to a questionnaire seeking their views on having to pay for library services. The results suggested that although users would not feel that they should pay for what were regarded as traditional core services, there was a willingness to consider paying for certain individual services based on choice and specific need. The authors suggest that countries such as the United Kingdom and the Netherlands have a more market-oriented approach, which is likely to encourage the introduction of more user payment-based services, although again protection is demanded for key core services in public libraries.

Attitudes to payment, whether direct or as part of an internal charging policy, have to be seen in the wider context of the impact of, and need for, specific information. Individuals may regularly or occasionally require certain data to support their work performance, or in relation to non-work activities and interests. The nature of their work or activities; the way in which they carry them out; their awareness and use of, as well as access to, the full range of information sources that would satisfy their needs, and of course the perceived cost in the time involved, will all contribute to their overall response to fees for the information itself and to the service that provides it.

Market research does not end with the launch of a service. Ongoing research of new markets and markets for new services may take place. Performances of new services also need to be assessed. A useful approach to this is offered by Ward (2000), who describes the investigation of the performance of a service by a survey of existing clients.

Results of the research

The results of your external market research should provide answers to the questions posed in the section on competition above. When these are co-ordinated with the results of the information audit and user needs analysis, you will be in a position to make an informed statement, backed by evidence, of your intentions. Evidence is likely to be crucial in getting top management approval for, and commitment to, the new method of operation and its resource implications.

Chapter 4

Initial planning

An early feature of the project will be a statement of its objectives and the methods and procedures by which these will be achieved, together with the resources necessary for success. Once a structured plan has been produced it will need the approval and support of top management before you can go further. This may be given on the understanding that regular feedback on progress will be made at all stages of the project prior to implementation. It may include a requirement for some sort of pilot to be carried out before full implementation. The main concern of top management is likely to relate to the efficient use of resources and improvements in services. Any proposal or presentation that you may need to make in support of the new service will have to be carefully prepared, to justify the costs and demonstrate the benefits. At this stage quantifiable justification, i.e. hard evidence, is what is required. How will you put together the necessary evidence and of what will it consist? Such evidence will provide the strong underpinning that your business plan will need.

The business plan

The business plan sets out the objectives of your proposal, clearly stating why it represents the best way forward, noting the benefits not just to individuals but also to the organisation as a whole, and, most importantly, how the objectives will be achieved in terms of procedures (see chapter 5) and resources. Resource considerations will include: costs and methods of cost recovery; staffing and skills requirements; location and access; amount and type of space; range of information sources and related equipment and software, not forgetting the cost of updating, upgrading and using these. Aspects of the business plan are now looked at in more detail, with brief definitions and explanations. MacKintosh (1999) provides a good introduction to elements of the business plan with specific reference to fee-based information services. If you need further advice on the broader framework of financial management within which this project might operate, consult the suggested further reading in chapter 9.

Costs

The elements which make up the total cost of any activity will include:

- staff costs based on time taken and the cost of that time to the employer
- purchase costs of source material (including subscriptions and usage rates for electronic sources)
- a percentage of the purchase and running costs of related equipment
- stationery and reproduction costs
- postage and telecommunications charges
- a percentage of overheads, e.g. light, heat and accommodation.

Overheads are a substantial part of a budget calculation for many fee-based services and they are calculated in different ways in different organisations. In particular, the methodology for attributing proportions of overheads to one part of the organisation or one part of the library and information service may vary; for example, it may be by staff numbers, size of budget, or floor space. Activity-based costing is a more sophisticated method of apportionment, which takes into account the variable nature of indirect costs depending on the mix and level of different activities by identifying cost drivers. The methodology should be agreed with the relevant authorities in the organisation and may make the difference between profit and loss in the financial out-turn. Since services within larger organisations may not be able to control their overheads, they may operate at a commercial disadvantage.

Cost recovery, surplus and profit

Cost recovery has a variety of meanings depending on the extent to which costs are identified for a particular cost centre, which might be an operational unit, service or activity. Cost recovery may denote:

- marginal cost recovery where only the additional direct costs of dealing with the extra fee-based work items are recovered but it is accepted that all the staff and other operating costs are already met from a mainstream budget
- that all direct costs of the fee-based services are recovered but the service makes no contribution to overheads, for example it uses existing accommodation without being charged rent
- comprehensive recovery of all costs, including overheads.

In the United States, fee-based services in libraries typically operate on principles of cost recovery according to Fong (1999, 63), who discusses the various definitions of the term.

A surplus is any excess of income over expenditure. For

a surplus to be regarded as a profit it has to be:

> a) intentionally created

and   b) available for distribution.

In certain types of institution a surplus is not available for distribution, for example in some charitable organisations any surplus must be re-invested in improvements which help those organisations to enhance their activities. For any service, whether or not it plans to make a profit, it is only prudent to plan for surpluses and these can accumulate through good management to fund growth and development and to provide for possible financial liabilities.

Several sources, including White (1992) and Abell et al. (1995), maintain that it is rare for a service not based wholly in the commercial environment to make a profit. However, a service need not make a profit to make a substantial financial contribution to its parent organisation. If overheads are fixed, a fee-based service which covers all its direct costs and contributes towards those overheads will reduce costs for the other parts of the organisation (see the Institute of Advanced Legal Studies case study in chapter 8).

Chargeable time

Chargeable time is the way in which client charges are calculated in a number of professions, for example accountancy or law, and is easily applied to LIS work. It involves each member of staff having a known hourly charge-out rate, usually based on salary. Records are kept of the amount of time spent on each piece of client-related work. These are then transferred to timesheets, which are passed at stated regular intervals to the central accounts department where they are co-ordinated and bills produced accordingly. Other, "non-chargeable", work is also recorded on the same basis and costs are passed on to internal departments. External clients and internal departments are allocated unique code numbers for these purposes.

Financial planning

As Corrall (2000, 165) advises in her "Money matters" chapter: "It is essential to note here that although financial plans will probably only emerge as formal budgets at a relatively late point in the planning process, financial issues need proper consideration throughout the strategic process, and any major strategic decisions must include consideration of financial implications at an early stage".

The whole area of financial management is one that is well worth revisiting at this stage. There are numerous general courses available, as well as management texts on the subject. In addition, there are some very helpful books and articles that have been written specifically with the LIS manager in mind. In addition to Corrall (2000) mentioned above, examples include McKay (2003), a concise guide, and Roberts (1998), the comprehensive text on financial management for library and information services.

Costing

Setting up a priced service involves deciding on a price for each particular service, for example research or document preparation, taking into account all the costs of providing it and whether or not you are aiming to make a profit. First you will be likely to focus on a breakdown of current costs within the existing budget to show how much expenditure is being made on which aspects of service provision. Consider whether the new approach will require the same type of expenditure or whether some features will be replaced by others, which may cost more or less than previously. You will then be able to draw up estimated overall costs for the future mix of service with a breakdown for each part of it, whether charge-based or not. This disaggregation of costs in order to establish the costs of individual activities or units within the library and information service is essentially an application of the programmed or functional budget approach described in McKay (2003) and more comprehensively in Roberts (1998). A further step is formally to link a budget that identifies the costs of a particular unit or service to measurable performance targets.

The estimates of costs should be as complete as possible and this is recognized as one of the most difficult tasks in the service sector, see Abell et al. (1995, 16-17). If full cost recovery is intended (see definitions above), but the full costs are underestimated, there is a danger that the parent organisation will be subsidising the service to the detriment of other services. The ironic situation may arise that a non-profit organisation may inadvertently subsidise a fee-based service designed to supplement its income.

Cost behaviour usually refers to the differential increases of the various cost elements of the operation as it grows. It is important to test your model of the costs of the service in several scenarios of growth. For example if you underestimate the cost of an element linked to the volume of usage, such as the amount of staff time used in an average enquiry, and consequently do not charge enough per enquiry, the shortfall will be magnified as the service grows. If the predicted costs include the whole salaries of a certain number of staff, there may be elasticity in their capacity to deal with enquiries up to a certain level but beyond that point costs will rise dramatically with the appointment of an additional member of staff.

In the management of a fee-based service it is crucial to have sufficient virement authority (discretion to apply expenditure flexibly between different budget heads, for example between staff and non-staff expenditure). It is also important to agree in advance with your institution how to account for any surplus or profit that is identified. If the institution does not allow the service or its parent library to retain any financial advantage or invest for the expansion of the service, or reduces other funding streams, then there will be little incentive to run a successful service.

Pricing

Based on your market research, you should draw up an estimate of income to be generated showing:

- total income likely to be derived from external clients

- a breakdown of that figure by estimates for each separate service

- costs to be recovered by passing on charges to internal clients, with a breakdown by department and by type of service used.

These estimates will be based on:

- analysis of previous and current use and any income generated to date

- perceived future use based on the above analysis and as expressed in user surveys

- trends in costs, e.g. salaries, information sources and equipment

- planned charges, which should take into account rates featuring in any existing internal charging policy, and the prices charged by competing external services.

Such figures will also be affected by your decision on whether you are aiming largely for profit or cost recovery. It is essential to have a clear understanding of the differences between these approaches. Thinking about the answers to the following questions might help inform your decision-making:

- Are you aiming to recover the costs incurred in carrying out certain activities across the board, e.g. photocopying, document delivery or online searching, or do you intend to focus on one or more specific subject areas in which you have expertise and turn each area of information provision into a self-financing unit?

- If the latter, will it be self-financing only in terms of recovering all costs, or will it generate a profit to be invested in the service's continued development?

- Is it more appropriate to state a standard charge or to give an individual quotation for each piece of work?

- Will you charge for a negative outcome, i.e. when you have seemingly explored all possible avenues but not been able to come up with the required information?

- What are the different elements that together make up the total overall cost?

- What exactly is chargeable time (see p. 30) and how would it work in your situation?

At this early stage you will be estimating income, but should have firmer figures for costs, based on current rates, such as salaries, book prices, journal and database subscriptions, telecommunications, postage, printing and reproduction. What you will be showing as estimated income could also be seen as your target. Even when the service is up and running and you have actual income to show, it is still good practice to continue to set targets as part of your long-term planning.

Pricing strategy will influence your income; a high price

could result in low usage, but a low price does not necessarily guarantee high usage. The user of a service may perceive its value as being cheapened by a low price, equating this with low quality. Tilson (1994) reported on pricing policies from a survey of London libraries in various sectors and, in addition, covered related issues such as attitude to pricing of different services. Corrall (2000, 186) identifies a range of internal and external issues, both tactical and strategic, relating to pricing decisions and says "Reliable information on service/product costs and an understanding of cost behaviour is essential for effective price setting, irrespective of the method adopted". In particular, she notes that there has been a general trend towards the creation of internal markets in companies and other institutions. The effect of devolved budgeting and service level agreements may, in effect, put the LIS in the position of providing a fee-based service see Lyon et al. (1998). The implications of these developments are profound and it is essential for LIS managers to be aware of the operation of the internal or transfer pricing system, which can be crucial to organisational effectiveness.

Having carried out your research and gathered the necessary data you will now need to consider the best way in which to put together the figures in support of your proposal to senior management. The way in which your arguments are presented and justified will require skills of presentation, persuasion and negotiation. A well-written and well-structured document presenting a plan based on logical arguments and hard facts will do a lot of the work for you.

Assessing the potential; operational considerations

Confidence in a service comes with experience of using and providing it, but at this early stage of planning a new service and new procedures experience is the one element not yet in place. Therefore there will be a degree of uncertainty in the minds of both the users and the provider as to how it might meet their long-term needs and objectives. As mentioned in chapter 3, any user surveys will have to be very carefully structured, whether by questionnaire or face-to-face interview, to determine the most viable range of services to be offered and appropriate prices and methods of charging for each.

So the LIS manager has two initial decisions to make: first, whether to pass on charges to internal users and, second, whether to offer fee-based services to external clients. The first decision is likely to relate to the internal procedures already in existence and whether charging is in operation. If so, it would seem to be a natural move for the LIS to participate. The second decision is perhaps more complex and involves an information-gathering exercise:

- concerning expressed user needs as indicated from an analysis of actual demand and use to date, and through user consultation
- relating to resources and your long-term objectives as addressed by the questions raised here
- considering the competition - after all, if there is a well-established and effective service already conveniently available will there be room for another one?

If your starting point is that you already have a useful collection of material in a specialist field, so why not make it more widely available and at the same time generate income to boost your budget, there are a number of questions to be asked and answered before going any further.

There will be questions relating to the material itself, for example:

- How comprehensive is it in terms of breadth of coverage?
- At what level is it aimed?
- How up to date or retrospective is it?

Then there are matters of staffing:

- Who will run the service?
- How many staff may be required?
- How will the new work patterns and demands relate to other duties?
- What subject knowledge and understanding will be required?
- What technical and administrative skills will be needed?
- Are there training implications?

Budgeting and planning considerations need to receive attention now to guarantee the long-term success of any such development:

- What will the set-up costs be as well as the longer-term running costs?
- Where will this stand in terms of meeting other objectives, priorities and responsibilities?
- What extras will be on offer to justify charging for an existing collection?
- Will any income generated be ploughed back into the specialist service or the overall LIS budget, or will it go into the organisational pot?

At the same time you must have identified any existing competing services, including those used by internal clients who may be approaching other sources directly and not through the LIS. You must also establish that there is a definite long-term demand from potential users in order to justify even the initial investment of money, time and effort. If you do go ahead there will of course be the promotional side to consider as well.

However, you may be starting from a different viewpoint - that of setting up an internal charging system as a means of passing charges on to other departments within your employing organisation. This would usually be related to the differing amounts of use made of your services but could be based on an equal amount being charged to each department for certain central services. The way in which the concept of internal charging is regarded as being feasible and acceptable is likely to depend largely on how much it is already part of overall organisational policy or planned as part of procedures to be applied across the board. The idea also needs to be sold to LIS staff as one that brings a variety of benefits and not just something that "adds to the paperwork" (see the CMS Cameron McKenna case study in chapter 8). Staff benefits to be promoted might include wider involvement, greater recognition, job satisfaction and enhancement, increased budgets, improved resources, even possibly greater job security as the service becomes regarded as indispensable.

Service delivery

Taking into account staffing and other resource implications, the method of delivery of the service requires careful consideration:

- Is the user expected to make a personal visit to use the service?
- Could the service be telephone-, fax- or email-based?
- In what format and in which languages can information be supplied?
- Can an electronic, or postal or a courier delivery service be offered?

- What sort of turn-around time will be required? (There may be performance measures or a service level agreement in place that will help to assess this and you should also ask questions about delivery time in your user surveys.)
- On what days and at what times can the service be accessed?

Payment

Having looked at delivery, you will also need to make a firm decision not only about pricing but also about payment. You will need policies on the form of payment: whether payment should be made by cash, cheque, credit or debit card, and on the timing of payment: whether payment should be made in advance, in arrears on receipt of an invoice, or as part of a subscription or a credit arrangement whereby clients pay a lump sum in advance and draw on the balance as required.

The methods adopted for charging may change the nature of the service. A subscription element may encourage the formation of a community of clients and long-term relationships, as indicated in the case study of the Institute of Advanced Legal Studies in chapter 8. Subscription charging gives greater financial stability by ensuring a more controllable cash flow and may be desirable when a service is set up, particularly if additional staff are being recruited. However, clients generally prefer pay-as-you-go schemes because they can more easily relate charges to usage and more easily pass on charges to other parts of their organisation or a further client. After a service is established, subscription charging may restrict the dynamic expansion of a service and deter new clients from trying the service.

Payment methods and procedures may be dictated by general policies operating throughout the organisation, so you will need to discuss this with the appropriate department to ensure consistency. See also the section on credit management in chapter 5.

Liability

Liability can arise in relation to the supply of information through breach of contract or through negligence; other legal considerations in the operation of the service are confidentiality - privacy or data protection - and defamation. (Copyright is dealt with in the next section.)

There is risk of liability even in well-run operations with established procedures for quality control. In general, creating and retaining accurate records is one of the prime requirements in establishing and demonstrating compliance in all fields of regulation. Professional indemnity insurance should be carefully considered with your employing organisation.

If a service is supplied to an external client for a fee, then there is a risk of liability for breach of contract. Risk can be minimised by explicit definitions in advance of the scope, level and response times or other performance criteria of the service. Internal service level agreements may not risk the same legal liability but equally benefit from being drawn up carefully; see Pantry and Griffiths (2001).

Service providers also owe a duty of care to their clients to meet their reasonable expectations of the service. Liability for negligence may arise, for example through an explicit or an implied warranty that information supplied is accurate, relevant and complete. A shared understanding of what can reasonably be expected of the service will minimise the risk. Disclaimers may not be an effective protection in some circumstances, in particular if a disclaimer is framed to exclude liability to an unreasonable extent.

In most organisations LIS staff are there to provide information, not advice, even if they hold specialist qualifications in the field in which advice is sought. The London Business School Information Service follows this policy saying, "We are not consultants and do not analyse the information we retrieve in any way. LBSIS staff all have postgraduate business information qualifications but are not economists or statisticians so it would not be appropriate, though if asked, we will offer opinions, based on our experience, of the resources and publications we use. For this reason our charges are much lower than those of consultants."

There is a requirement for confidentiality both in terms of professional ethics and in terms of the law. For example, it may cause serious harm to a client's business if their need for particular information were communicated to a third party, such as to another client asking for the same information. In the United Kingdom the Data Protection Act 1998, as amended by the Freedom of Information Act 2000, regulates the storage and processing of personal data and this affects client databases and record keeping (see chapter 6). The Information Commissioner (see Appendix for contact details) publishes legal guidance, which is freely available on the web.

Liability may also arise for defamatory statements, made in writing or orally, where opinions or inaccurate facts are expressed. The statement needs to be "published" but this has a broad interpretation and great care should be taken even on in-house email systems.

McKenzie provides a brief introduction to liability for information provision in Scammell (2001, 466-474) and there is a fuller introduction in Mowat (1998) who suggests management practices to minimise risk. There are notes of relevant legal developments in the professional press, and a regular column by Oppenheim in the *Journal of Information Science*.

Copyright

Another important consideration is compliance with the current copyright regime and the licensing terms for printed and electronic products. Suppliers of information services should be fully conversant with the requirements and the possible interpretations in order to identify, for example, when permissions may be required, when a fee may be payable to the copyright owner, and where fair dealing and other exceptions may apply. There is an extensive literature, mainly published by the library professional organisations, which employ copyright advisers. Pedley (2000) is a concise and practical guide and Cornish (2001) takes the form of answers to "frequently asked questions". The Chartered Institute of Library and Information Professionals publishes guides, including Norman (1999) to copyright in industrial and commercial libraries. Consult the comprehensive text by Wall (2000) as a regular source of reference for checking the detail of the legislation and its possible interpretation.

Copyright regulation is changing quite quickly, particularly with the impact of European Union measures, and the professional literature should be scanned for developments. Changes to the copyright regime are imminent to reduce the scope of the fair dealing exception, which at the time of writing allows single copies of limited extent for "research and private study". The relevant new provisions are contained in a European directive, see European Union (2001), and are currently intended to be transposed into UK law by August 2003. These changes will affect individuals and information services which make copies under library privilege for researchers, external or internal, who then use copies directly or indirectly for commercial purposes. Any copying for commercial research will need permission from the copyright holder and licensing through a mandated agency is probably the only viable way to achieve this if you intend to copy from a range of publications. The United Kingdom Patent Office website at http://www.patent.gov.uk/copy/index.htm contains details of the provisions, their effect and the progress of implementation as well as a general introduction to copyright and a list of current legislation.

The Copyright Licensing Agency acts as an agent for many publishers in administering copyright licensing fees and offers a range of leaflets on its services and extensive information on its website (see Appendix for contact details). The Copyright Licensing Agency does not offer a comprehensive service and there are other organisations which offer licences for particular materials, for example the Newspaper Licensing Agency (see Appendix for contact details).

Feasibility testing

At this stage you should be planning your methods of testing the feasibility of the priced service. Your earlier consultation with users about their existing and perceived future information needs should have given you a good insight into the probable response to the new service and to the concept of it being fee-based. The market research into other similar, possibly competing, services will have added to this. However, it could be well worthwhile testing the service "for real" with a pilot study. This involves selecting a target group - perhaps one of those used in the client surveys - telling its members what is on offer, how it will work and how valuable their participation will be. Run it over a set period of time, probably not more than a few months, and build in mechanisms for regular monitoring and feedback. This may be in the form of feedback slips, email communications, brief questionnaires or user review meetings. Whichever form you choose make sure that it will be quick and easy for the user to respond and that you only ask for information essential to the decision-making - the "need to know" and not the "nice to know" approach.

User perceptions and expectations, as well as the actual delivery of the service, can have a considerable impact on the successful implementation of a charging policy. These relate strongly to the way in which the value of the service itself and the charging procedures have been presented. The promotion of services is discussed in chapter 6; but before promoting services, basic procedures must be put into place.

Chapter 5

Procedures, documentation and control

By now you should have been able to draw up a clear statement of *what* you want to happen and *when*. The next step is to decide *how* it should happen. Efficient procedures will underpin the successful implementation of any charging policy. Procedures will range over records and administration to the behavioural aspects of service provision. For example, organisations seeking recognition in relation to formal standards of quality assurance such as BS/EN/ISO9000 (formerly BS5750 in the United Kingdom) may have already introduced various codes of practice involving matters such as dress and preferred ways of communicating with clients - external and internal - as well as standard administrative procedures. Where quality assurance or quality management policies exist these must be taken into account in your planning and the standard procedures followed, for example recording of costs, invoicing, receipt and acknowledgement of payment. This can prove to be a very helpful starting point, providing focus and direction for other procedures that you may need to devise. If such policies and procedures do not exist within your own employing organisation, it could be useful to discuss ways of handling certain aspects of charging with LIS managers in other institutions, always bearing in mind the possibly sensitive or confidential nature of such developments.

Automation

Many aspects of the administration of fee-based services are suitable for automation. The maintenance of client records, enquiry tracking and order fulfilment can be automated, as Gee and Whittle (1996) describe in a discussion of use at the Institute of Advanced Legal Studies. Database systems can facilitate mailings and promotional activities, generate invoices, and produce valuable itemised reports on services supplied enabling clients to identify individual requests. Management information can assist in quality control because throughput and performance levels can be monitored and can provide valuable input to development planning by identifying trends. Recent developments include employing online ordering and tracking systems, see Ward et al. (1999, 109). Automation, of course, complements but does not replace access to human expertise, which is often the greatest asset of the service provider in a library and information service.

Manual of procedures

If a manual of procedures does not already exist, now is the time to create one. There needs to be a clear statement of how the charging policy operates, which services are chargeable, to whom and how. Operations and related procedures at each stage of the process should be described and copies of relevant documentation included. Include examples of related printed material, with details of how this was produced - internally or by outside printers - a contact name, production schedule (who needs to do what, by when, to achieve a desired delivery date) and costs. This will be useful for future decision-making. All staff should be encouraged to regard the manual as a valuable point of reference and to contribute to it as part of a co-ordinated process, so that the manual develops in parallel with the service. Staff may still find it valuable to have a hard copy version of the manual for quick reference but the contents are best stored in computer form for ease of updating and amendment, and for consultation on-screen. The material is ideal for an institutional intranet.

Enquiry record

What procedures and records will be required? If the service is largely an enquiry-based one, then you are likely to have the first item already in frequent use: the enquiry record. It is essential as a clear statement of what is required, by whom and when; it may cover details of sources used, and should show the name of the member of staff handling the enquiry for future follow-up.

For the purposes of charging, a number of further headings can be added to show the time taken, client name and contact details, as well as any charge code applied. You will also need to take account of any constraints over and above that of the deadline, for example any predetermined financial limit that the user is not prepared to exceed. In this case, the enquirer may wish to have an interim progress report to see what has been produced to date and at what cost, so put in another heading to cover this. You should also establish and note the preferred form in which the client wants the information to be presented (in line with what you can offer), for instance, in electronic form compatible with particular software, as OHP transparencies or as a bound report, and the required method of delivery, such as email, post or courier. Allow for the delivery method in your pricing calculation. As well as providing a record, the various headings can act as a useful reminder for you about the information you require from the client at the outset. Use your computer to try out various formats until you have one that gives you the layout that best suits the purpose. You will then be able to store it and adapt as necessary at a later stage. File a copy of the enquiry form in the manual of procedures with an accompanying note, expanding as necessary on each heading, its purpose and the method of completion.

Terms of business

It is at the initial enquiry stage that you should inform the client of any legal or contractual arrangements, such as liability, payment terms or copyright. It helps to have a carefully prepared leaflet setting out your terms of business; it is advisable to seek legal advice on this through your organisation's own advisers. Service level agreements are seen largely as internal contracts, reached by agreement with internal users. However, for external clients you may wish to draw up a code that will set out the level of service that they can expect, such as the length of time it will take for initial response, whether answering the telephone or acknowledging a written or electronic communication; and for final response, such as providing information or producing a report. Pantry and Griffiths (2001) give details of preparing and implementing service level agreements, dealing with issues of quality and charging; their advice is equally useful for drawing up agreements with external clients.

Although the service needs to generate business, it is important to reject work if it goes beyond the scope or expertise of the service. As Abell et al. (1995, 24) note: "It is extremely important in the information business to learn to say no".

Client communication procedures

In the manual of procedures include a statement of standard practice about the way in which communication is made with the client. This will cover method - whether by letter, telephone or email - and style, for instance, degree of formality and mode of address. Communications skills training will help in this and if your organisation is pursuing a strategy of quality management there should be an accepted standard of operation set out for all departments and functions in the quality manual. Include a note about the preferred style of communicating the enquiry response to clients and the way in which this response should be recorded internally. The timing of interim and progress reports needs to be stated, also the approach to be taken to inform the enquirer of a negative outcome. The way in which a message is communicated, the words used and tone adopted, will have considerable impact on the way in which it is accepted by the recipient.

Telephone calls must be logged if charges are to be passed on, but this may already be done automatically across the organisation. If not, you will need to decide how and what to record. This will depend on whether you intend to charge for the total cost of all calls made on behalf of each client, or to exempt local calls or those of a very short duration; your policy must be stated in your terms of business. However, you may decide not to pass on the costs of any calls. Although numerous short calls can add up to a considerable expenditure overall, you may still feel that it would not be appropriate to pass on what might be regarded by the client as unreasonable or insignificant charges. It is something that you will have to weigh up in terms of public relations as well as in financial terms and take this into account in your decision-making.

Financial procedures and records

You will need a clear statement in the manual about the various charges made and how these were arrived at, so that all staff will be able to understand the pricing structure and the reasoning behind it. This will enable staff to answer questions that may be put to them by the enquirer. List all the charges for different aspects of the service, including those made for a negative outcome, and the way in which to estimate individual tailor-made requests if a standard set charge is not to be used. To assist internal administration, include a list of the various client codes for accounting purposes.

Set out other financial procedures and records in this section, with details of methods of payment, invoicing and receipt procedures and file a copy of the terms of business here. If invoicing is to be carried out by LIS staff, and not handled centrally, it is worth drawing up a sample standard invoice showing the amount of detail to be itemised and the preferred layout. It is always worth putting a note of the required payment date at the bottom of the invoice, for example: "Payment should be made within 30 days." If all payments have to be made in advance, LIS staff may have to be authorized by the head of finance or other senior manager to handle such payments. Some training might also be necessary.

Credit management

Getting people to pay for something that they have already received is not always easy; we all know how invoices get pushed to the bottom of the pile, left in the pending tray, or are thought to have been passed to someone else. Always send out invoices promptly, clearly stating payment terms. As soon as payment is received it must be matched against the original copy invoice, flagging unpaid invoices in some convenient way to enable the customer to be "chased" for payment.

If LIS staff have responsibility not only for calculating charges for work and invoicing external clients, but also for chasing payments that are overdue, there are behavioural considerations to be addressed: be prepared, have all the facts to hand, be positive, be persistent, remain polite but firm - after all you would prefer to keep the business. Training will help, but so will clearly stated terms of business and internal procedures. You will need to establish a follow-up procedure in terms of timing, approach and recording, and decide whether one member of staff has responsibility for this area or whether the person handling that client enquiry should also manage the financial side. If chasing is done by telephone, confirm what has been agreed in writing: this may take the form of a duplicate invoice with a covering note, or a letter confirming a new credit limit or existing balance.

It is good practice to set agreed credit limits with clients - you won't want these to be too low as less credit means less potential usage - but if there is an agreed limit both parties are aware of that agreement. Use credit as a positive marketing tool - it has certainly been used to great effect in the credit card business. This is a definite benefit for clients and you want them to make maximum use of the service.

All these procedures will have to be checked with overall organisational policies of credit management and control.

Budgetary control

Regular monitoring of the budget to ensure that financial objectives are being met is central to measuring progress and likely to be required as part of overall organisational financial control. Therefore procedures may already be in place for this, but you will still need to have a section on it in the manual. This should describe how often monitoring takes place, how the process operates, and who is responsible for carrying it out. If you want to be able to separate out the administrative costs and the income generated for each charged service, or the costs transferred to each internal department, the most common means of achieving such a distinction is to set up a separate budget code or cost centre for each. This can easily be done using a spreadsheet package, or even manually, and will more than repay any time invested in setting up the system. It will enable you to see at a glance the current financial state of the charged part of the total LIS activity, how it is matching up to your estimates and whether any change of direction is required. This will also inform your longer-term overall planning. Make a note of any systems file names which relate to the fee-based service and its operation.

Staff

Staff responsibilities should be clearly defined and stated. Note common areas of activity within the charged service in which everyone participates, as well as areas of special responsibility which may relate to, for example, particular subject knowledge or to technical expertise or administrative skills. It will be helpful to list any courses and other training activities that have been identified as having relevance to particular aspects of charged services, with a note of possible providers and costs. An ongoing programme of staff development (see chapter 2, "Staff training needs") will be an integral part of maintaining the service and could also prove useful in identifying opportunities for career development and for future staff planning. In this section on staff include a note of the chargeout rates for respective grades, with the period of time to which they apply, and amend these if appropriate, for example as rates change elsewhere in the organisation or if posts are regraded. Consistently high levels of service require adequate staffing levels and expertise in the delivery of the services but also in management. The additional load on senior management is often over-looked in planning and costing fee-based services. It should be emphasized that throughout this section reference should be made in your documentation to individual posts, rather than to named members of staff.

Levels of service often depend on a certain speed of response; this may be an explicit guarantee or it may be implicit in the contract with the client. Maintaining speedy services throughout advertised hours with fluctuating levels of demand requires careful administration and flexibility in managing staff resources, particularly in a small unit. It may be necessary to draw staff from elsewhere in the organisation if the service is based in a larger LIS.

If the services are provided within a larger LIS you will need to decide whether the unit will be run by dedicated staff or whether to draw some or all of the staff by rota from the staff of the parent LIS. Dedicated staff may best co-ordinate and be responsible for the performance of regularly used services. However, a separate unit may develop a separate ethos and become estranged from the parent LIS and its staff. Depending on its focus, a fee-based service may also need to draw on the expertise of the wider group of staff. This runs the risk of distracting staff from their normal duties unless their contribution is closely defined. However, it may also provide additional challenges and job satisfaction and may reinforce user focus in the provision of services throughout the LIS.

Marketing and promotion procedures

You will need to set out your marketing and promotion strategy with its rationale. It will be as important in future planning to know why you chose not to pursue certain tactics as to know the reasons for pursuing others. It has already been suggested that examples of your promotional literature should be included in the manual. It could also be worth filing examples of the publicity material produced by those running similar services, along with other information that you may have collected on possible competitors as part of your initial market research. This will be useful in the continuous monitoring of your own position in the market. Procedures and methods of carrying out such monitoring need to be described, as well as the specific monitoring responsibilities of individual post-holders who might be assigned, for example, to cover specific subject areas or sections of the press.

The list of core procedures and records above will apply to most charged services, but there may be additional ones that you should include, either because they form part of overall organisational standards and methods of operating, or because they relate to one or more specialised services that you offer. Make an entry for each in the manual. The sequence and layout of entries or sections within the printed manual must be one that makes it quick and easy to use. An alphabetical sequence by keyword with cross references has been used successfully and so has an alphabetical arrangement with a covering index - all easy to develop using appropriate software. Make descriptions of procedures clear and concise; there is no room for ambiguity - this is the manual on which the successful operation of your service depends.

Chapter 6

Marketing and promotion

We should all promote our libraries and information services constantly, whether or not we make a charge to the user. Users and potential users need to be made aware of, and kept up to date with, the range of services available to them. However, you also need to inform your client base of any changes in the procedures that underpin the services. Make internal clients aware of the fact that charges are going to be passed on to departments or individuals, and give a clear reason for the change in procedure: that it is part of a more efficient management and financial planning approach. If you plan to introduce any internal service level agreement or statement of service standards, it would be appropriate at the same time to set out the new charging arrangements and to promote any new methods of information provision. In the case of charging external clients you must be able to set the notion of charging against the perceived additional benefits to the user of any new or enhanced service. Marketing strategy and marketing action plans are explained in a practical and concise way in Coote and Batchelor (1997).

There are a number of methods of communicating with internal and external clients. You will have to decide, given the mix of your client base, just what sort of marketing and promotion techniques would be most appropriate and what kind of image you are aiming to present:

do you need a trademark, an appropriate name or logo? Budget constraints may mean that you would want to produce a common core of publicity material so that it could be used internally and externally, or easily adapted to cover both, by using separate supplementary inserts for "free" and charged services.

Websites

The potential of a website in promoting your service has been realised by libraries and information centres in many sectors. However, as already noted, a website needs to be designed carefully, with clear and precise signposts to its various sections. Use concise, plain language and appropriate images - don't overdo the clever moving images as they can be irritating and time-consuming distractions. Ensure that the site is usable by visitors who do not have the most recent browser software, and give consideration to speed of loading and supported features. A general email address should be established for the service but in addition websites may incorporate an online form for further information, registration, and placing requests or bookings.

An excellent example of a well-produced website is BestofBiz.com, which won the 2001 LA/PR award. As well as providing access to a wide range of information it also acts as a considerable promotional tool for the London Business School Information Service (see Appendix for contact details). Although BestofBiz.com is a free business and management portal, and a research tool in its own right, it also advertises the fee-based services of the London Business School Information Service, a service separate from the School's library. The site has been promoted in various ways, taking both a technical and an incentive-based approach. It was registered with the major search engines and comprehensively meta-tagged to ensure that business researchers would visit BestofBiz. Small, engraved clocks provided the incentive to early membership and were sent out to the first people to join. BestofBiz pens, carrier bags and bookmarks are widely distributed, and posters and brochures are displayed in the LBS library. The site has been demonstrated at various events at the LBS, presentations made at a number of international conferences and exhibitions, and articles written for in-house and external publications. Registered users are regularly informed of enhancements by email, which further promotes the service. Interestingly, as with the BRIS case study in chapter 8, the development of the site involved the use of LBS library staff as well as those of the LBSIS, with their range of different but complementary skills.

Publications

Don't forget the usefulness of simple, paper-based publications that might already exist, such as guides to the service, newsletters, bulletins and reading lists. You could take the opportunity to revise and sharpen the focus of some of these existing materials; for example, why not produce a quick guide to the LIS as an insert for a personal organiser or course folder? It could just include key facts such as postal, website and email addresses, telephone and fax numbers, hours of opening and availability, contact names, main services and a small diagram showing location.

Every item of publicity will make a visual impact, even before the reader starts to look at the content, so it is worth passing proposed publicity material around to colleagues outside the LIS for objective comment. Is the colour right? What about the paper type and size? Would it look better if professionally printed rather than produced in-house? If on the web, does it have visual appeal? Then look at the content - is the writing clear and the style interesting? Does it contain the right amount of information? Is the information aimed at the user, addressing their needs? In short, are you getting the message across? These are all questions you should ask in relation to producing any new publicity material, whether revised or starting from scratch. If you intend to use such material as part of a promotional mailing, then the size (to fit standard envelopes) and weight (its effect on the cost of postage) will also be important considerations.

Direct marketing

Mailshots require careful consideration not only in terms of cost, but also with regard to the law concerning advertising and unsolicited mail. There is a range of UK statutes and regulations, and also European legislation, bearing on advertising, in addition to the law on matters such as contract, negligence, defamation and intellectual property. There is a self-regulatory structure for advertising in the United Kingdom and this is the best avenue for investigation. The Committee of Advertising Practice (CAP) draws up, revises and enforces the British Codes of Advertising and Sales Promotion, which are the rules that apply to non-broadcast advertising in the United Kingdom. The UK Advertising Standards Authority (ASA) is the independent body that endorses and administers the Codes. The Codes give straightforward guidance on all aspects of advertising, including direct marketing. They are available to read, search and download from the websites of both organisations. On the ASA website you can register a profile for an email alerting service for future developments relevant to your interests. See the Appendix for contact details for both bodies and for the code see Advertising Standards Authority (2003) in the list of ref-

erences and further reading in chapter 9. The requirements for promotional mailings to and from other countries may need to be checked, and both the above organisations maintain relationships with regulatory bodies
in other countries and umbrella federations; CAP and
ASA provide website links to those organisations. The
Direct Marketing Association (UK) Ltd is a membership
association which promulgates its own codes of practice
and best practice guidelines, and gives helpful advice
on direct mailing on its website (see Appendix for contact details).

Data protection

Another legal aspect which you need to check concerns
data protection or privacy legislation in relation to the
maintenance of personal data, including mailing lists. In
the United Kingdom the holding and processing of personal data is regulated by the Data Protection Act 1998,
as amended by the Freedom of Information Act 2000.
Guidance on the current position can be obtained from
the UK's Information Commissioner (see Appendix for
contact details), formerly the Data Protection Registrar.
Considerable information is available on the official
website, including a guide of over 100 pages revised
most recently in 2001, which is free to download, and
there is a chapter on the subject by Amanda McKenzie in
Scammell (2001, 451-465). It should be noted that the legislation now covers data held in relevant manual filing
systems, not just computerised records. Organisations
register with the Information Commissioner and declare
the purposes for which they keep personal data and each
organisation appoints a member of staff as a data protection officer. It would be wise, in the first instance, to talk
to the person with responsibility for these matters in
your organisation to ensure that you are aware of the
requirements.

Other promotional activities

Other printed material could include advertisements in newspapers and journals, as well as notices and posters. Make a much more structured use of notice boards. These should be appropriately situated and material on them arranged with care, perhaps grouped under headings and labelled accordingly. Libraries have sometimes made use of specially printed bookmarks and labels to carry a marketing message, however brief. An easily identifiable logo on all communications can have quite an influence in terms of increasing product awareness and recognition. Look out for new directories in which you could get a listing, or journals that carry regular features in your field of activity. Whatever method you choose, always make sure that all items carry your organisation's name and contact number, so that interested parties can follow up and make contact. Remember that a simple printed communication instantly presents your message to potential users; without them having to look for it, or even know about it beforehand.

The impact of a well-designed publicity leaflet or brochure can be considerable, and the leaflet needs to be kept under constant review to ensure that the style as well as the content is current. The leaflet setting out your terms of business is also a promotional document of which maximum use should be made. It should be sent to initial enquirers who ask about the service, along with an accompanying letter. Send leaflets and brochures out with any press releases to journals, newspapers or even to radio and TV stations. See Coote and Batchelor (1997) for more on press releases and other promotional activities. Brochures can be displayed in your reception area and in those of other organisations with whom you have an appropriate working relationship, for example chambers of commerce or local public libraries, as well as at conferences or exhibitions. When you visit any of these don't forget or underestimate the usefulness of the business card as a promotional tool.

Promotional activities increasingly involve technology. You may produce demonstration diskettes or CDs, which potential users can test for themselves. Alternatively you could have a promotional film or video made, but do seek professional assistance in this - the "home movie" usually looks to be just that, whereas you are trying to sell a professional service. The dramatic increase in the use of, and access to, worldwide computer networks offers boundless possibilities in terms of reaching and communicating with potential and existing users, and already plays a key part in information exchange and provision in a variety of organisations, especially those with international interests.

Another widely used method of publicising services is the oral presentation, which again can be used internally and externally, supported by your promotional material. Strong communication skills are essential with an appreciation of what makes an effective presentation. Tailoring the talk to the audience, providing the opportunity for questions to be asked, good timing, well-produced visual aids and a comfortable and well-arranged venue, free from distraction, are all important. This method requires practice, preferably in front of a group of colleagues who are willing and able to make constructive criticism, before the talk is launched on the intended audience. As well as informal feedback of this kind, some formal training might be required.

Chapter 7

Conclusions

How do you take the service forward, ensuring that it continues to meet present needs, but does not miss out on future opportunities and changing requirements?

First, you need to carry out market research continuously, so that you are alert to, and can act on, opportunities to introduce additional services or to change existing ones. Each change that you make, however small, will give you another reason to make contact with clients, and scope for further marketing and promotion. You and your staff will have to keep up to date with developments in your geographical area of operation as well as in your subject field.

Don't overlook the fact that external services could be competitors for your internal clients as well as for those outside, so keeping a close eye on such developments is important. The national and local business press, as well as IT and LIS journals, will help in this, especially in the case of services to external clients. Press monitoring can be allocated to specific members of the team, with each member taking responsibility for a certain subject area or geographical region. It will help ensure that full use is made of staff expertise, as well as continuing to create a strong sense of involvement and responsibility for each staff member's role in the business. Carry out daily press scanning and monitoring, with prompt action on the output while the opportunity is still there. This will help develop staff awareness of what is going on outside the immediate work environment and keep staff in touch with the world in which their clients are operating - this is essential if alertness to opportunity is to be developed and maintained.

Put performance measures in place so you can assess accurately how the service is proceeding, where its areas of success lie, and where it might improve. Personal performance targets for staff could also be introduced to measure particular features of their work which relate to the priced service. Staff may have taken on extra areas of responsibility, as well as meeting additional and different demands. Present this in a non-threatening way, as a positive measure, a way of recognizing what the staff have achieved. After all, staff form a vital part of the service and you will want them to know how well they are doing and how much their contribution is valued. This can provide a strong motivator to further achievement.

The brainstorming sessions which helped you with the initial planning could usefully be continued, forming part of regular service reviews. Regard these as team meetings, at which solutions can be found through problem sharing, and new ideas can be put forward for discussion. These may be about revising procedures and prices, as well as creating additional services.

You will need continued and regular contact with existing clients, measuring satisfaction and establishing changing needs. Think carefully about the way in which you pursue this, striking a balance in terms of frequency and demands on user time against your need for specific feedback. It is best to set expectations at the start that some sort of follow-up is likely to take place and what form this might take. There are some suggestions of ways of obtaining a response in chapter 3.

Continuous monitoring, commercial acumen, an awareness of the part that your service can play both within and outside your own organisation, linked to subject knowledge and professional standards and practice, will all play a crucial part in helping you to assess the position of your service in the market and to assist in planning its future direction and continued success. This is well illustrated in the case studies that follow.

Chapter 8

Case studies

To illustrate the type of decisions to be made at policy and operational levels, four organisations of different kinds and with varying objectives were invited to describe from their own experiences certain aspects of introducing and running a fee-based service. All the case studies demonstrate the importance of ongoing review and the requirement to be able to respond to constantly changing needs and demands.

8.1 CMS Cameron McKenna (Solicitors)

CMS Cameron McKenna is an international law firm, and the library and information service (LIS) serves the information needs of the whole firm. As a service within a commercial entity the primary function of the LIS is to fulfil the requirements of the business. Unlike public or government libraries we have a defined audience: the members of the firm. As a library we use outside sources such as the Institute of Advanced Legal Studies, Information for Business, the Law Society, the British Library, online databases, CD-ROMs and commercial Internet databases, all of which involve costs.

It is not the prime objective of our LIS to run a "priced service" marketed to the general public; however, as most commercial organisations find, an opportunity to reduce overheads and increase income is an opportunity not to be missed. The library in any law firm is a commercial concern, continually justifying its existence; generating income is an excellent means of placing a value on the service. Charging for a service raises the profile of that service to the partners and fee earners of the firm while also helping the budgetary position of the department. It is always easier to promote the library or argue for funds when a monetary value can be attached to the performance of the department. This source of perceived income has become increasingly important in recent years and now forms a crucial part of our budgetary management.

There are two main categories of charging within the LIS at CMS Cameron McKenna: charging for time and charging for information. We carry out online searches, supply documents and photocopies, and provide external services.

Charging for time

Charging for time has long been standard practice for professionals such as accountants and lawyers yet it has only been adopted in law firm libraries in the last 12-15 years. In the United States many legal practices have run their libraries as profit centres for decades, yet in the United Kingdom charging for library time has been surprisingly slow to develop. Traditionally, UK law firm libraries were viewed as a necessary overhead and normally considered as a service or administrative department. This is exemplified by the fact that most UK law firms refer to solicitors as "fee earners" - the ones bringing in the money - not a term considered appropriate for librarians. Many law firms continue to see libraries as an overhead and undervalue them, tending to consider them as areas to cut when cost reductions are necessary and certainly not as fee-earning departments.

CMS Cameron McKenna introduced charging for LIS time in the early 1990s and various lessons have been learned since then. Charging certainly has a number of advantages, but it can also have some disadvantages. Some of the disadvantages include the time-consuming administration of recharging and the initial challenge of changing the perceptions of our immediate clients - the fee earners of the firm. The LIS is traditionally viewed as being a freely available service, rather than one that is a chargeable resource in the same way that solicitors' time is chargeable. The value of correct and comprehensive information is fundamental to the provision of a legal service, but this is not necessarily perceived by lawyers and so has to be proven.

At CMS Cameron McKenna only client chargeable time is recharged; time spent on research for practice development, such as marketing information, is recorded for statistical purposes, but treated as an overhead. Clients are charged specifically for the costs of the service used for that client work. To make this feasible, only research taking over 10 minutes is recharged; quick enquiries such as locating a case report or piece of legislation are recorded for statistical purposes only. As a management tool, the details of how time is spent within the LIS is useful information for internal audits, whether it is chargeable or not, allowing analysis of usage by the various practice areas within the firm, as well as by the nature of the research.

Administration of time charging was originally carried out using paper forms. All library enquiries are entered onto numbered enquiry sheets in tear-off pads. These enquiry sheets serve several purposes, prompting the librarian for relevant details, such as deadline and client matter to be charged as well as providing a column to record the time spent on the query. Details of what the enquiry was and what sources were used are noted, which is a useful quality assurance tool regardless of whether the time is recharged. An example is shown in Figure 8.1.1.

cameron mcKenna	CMS Cameron McKenna	
Library **Mitre House**		Enquiry Form No. 39929

Enquirer:	Client/Account Name:		Date received:
On behalf of:	Matter:		Time received:
	Computer No:		Deadline:
Received by:		Handled by:	Date satisfied:

ENQUIRY:	Time Spent:	
	Hrs.	Mins

SOURCES TRIED AND
RESULTS:

Total this page		
Total overleaf		

(Supplementary page overleaf) | Total time | | |

* The term 'members' includes registered students of the Institute

Figure 8.1.1: CMS Cameron McKenna library enquiry form

At the end of each week the information on each client chargeable enquiry sheet is entered onto a summary sheet, recording the client and matter number, the fee earner concerned, the amount of time spent, the enquiry sheet number and brief identifying details of the enquiry. This summary is then sent to the accounts department to be entered onto the library cost recovery budget as well as being allocated to the relevant client bills, although the final decision on whether the amount can be charged to the client rests with the client partner. The original sheets are retained in numerical order, providing details if there is any query on the charge. Although some time recharged in this way may be written off by the client partner, the library cost recovery budget enables analysis of information work, and the amounts which could have been raised.

In the past, the use of forms has made the administration of this system as quick and painless as possible. In 2002 we joined the electronic time-recording system used within the firm by fee earners for the summary and recharge stage. This enables transparency of charges throughout the firm, with details immediately visible on client records. However, the paper enquiry forms have quality process functions beyond time charging, and the low tech advantage of being easy to pick up and take anywhere, to note details of an enquiry while using one of the reference sources.

Charging for information

Charging for information has always been less controversial for libraries than charging for time. Online searches have long been an easily identifiable cost and one of the first areas where charges were passed on in most libraries. In this regard the law firm library is probably not that different from many other libraries. The fact that we are not commercial information brokers is reflected in our online contracts, and we would not be able to sell such online services directly to external bodies. However, research carried out for our clients as part of the legal service can be recharged to the client together with the legal advice.

CMS Cameron McKenna uses a specific form - this time in triplicate for ease of administration. This form provides prompts for the client's name, database used and length of time spent online; an example is shown in Figure 8.1.2. One copy is sent to the accounts department, one to the fee earner for their records and one is retained for queries and usage analysis.

In a similar manner, we incur costs when using external bodies, so these are also relatively easy to identify and recover. A corresponding form is used for external services, such as BLDSC (British Library Document Supply Centre), IALS (Institute of Advanced Legal Studies) and the Law Society, which provides prompts for the required details, and is easily distributed to all necessary parties.

Current development

Law firms have gradually been moving away from charging hourly rates for certain work towards making increasing use of all-inclusive packages. Library services can be used in such deals as a value-added incentive to the prospective client - as long as the LIS provides a good service. The library as a business unit receives no individual profit in recharging services under such deals; rather, it is a benefit gained by the whole firm. Recording of time is still carried out as an internal audit to see what resources go into a particular package.

As a result there is a need to market the LIS not just to the fee earners but also to the clients, providing details of services and resources available, service levels such as quality and speed of research, and professional expertise. It is important to respond to changing needs and

DATABASE SEARCH FORM

TIME RECORDER/
STAFF MEMBER
REQUESTING SEARCH

DEPT

PERSON UNDERTAKING
SEARCH (IF NOT SAME
AS ABOVE

DATE

The cost of this search is chargeable to the file indicated below

COMPUTER NO.

CLIENT

MATTER

DATABASE(S) SEARCHED

LEXIS	LEXIS/NEXIS	DOW JONES	
DIALOG	REUTERS	LAWTEL	
CCN	DUN & BRADSTREET	OTHER DATABASE (SPECIFY BELOW)	
DATASTAR	JUSTIS ONLINE		
NEW LAW	PERFECT INFORMATION		

SEARCH REQUEST

TIME SPENT ONLINE

INFORMATION DEPT. USE ONLY

COST OF SEARCH   INFO. DEPT COPY

* The term 'members' includes registered students of the Institute

Figure 8.1.2: CMS Cameron McKenna database enquiry form

demands; charging is constantly monitored and adapted for the changing nature of the work as individual clients can have very different requirements. Regular client liaison for the LIS in such situations now has to be held alongside the fee earner client liaison, leading to a much closer relationship to the business of the firm. This has the advantage of increasing the internal perception of the LIS, a very positive step in any organisation.

Resource implications

If LIS managers are not involved directly with the initial marketing contact for use of library facilities, resource implications can often be overlooked. The administrative and budgetary burden is considerable. There are also issues of staff training and awareness of the clients involved. These increases in work levels are not necessarily accompanied by an increase in staffing levels; a situation that is familiar to all libraries. Ideally, such issues should be addressed before the service is offered, as well as being constantly reviewed. Unfortunately we do not always live in an ideal world.

Marketing

The target market for the LIS within a law firm is well defined: the firm and its clients. However, promotion is still important. Internally, every contact with a fee earner is a marketing exercise, illustrating what the LIS can do for the firm. The LIS is increasingly involved in the marketing of the whole firm, and quality and speed of response is a prerequisite. Marketing documentation needs to be produced and included in appropriate client materials, quite separately from the normal internal guides, resource details and documentation of the department. The professional manner in which enquiries are handled by the service can have a large impact on a client's impression of the firm.

Strategic objectives

With the increased use of all-inclusive packages, there can be some problems of conflicting priorities. Clients may be given promises of specific performance levels, such as response times, and partners within the firm have their own expectations. If staffing levels are such that the same member of staff has to deal with a partner's demands for research within an immediate time scale and a direct client enquiry is received at the same time, which enquiry takes precedence? Performance levels have to be maintained for this external audience as well as for the firm itself.

Offering library and information services to clients raises questions about whether the LIS is reducing a client's need to use the solicitors themselves for non-interpretative matters; that could possibly mean fewer fees for the "fee earners". Strategic objectives should be carefully examined within the firm to ensure that a successful and beneficial relationship with clients is maintained, with maximum benefit to the firm. If the profile of the LIS is improved as part of the process, that is a considerable benefit.

The future

The increased marketing of legal services electronically will have an impact on the way in which we charge for information in the future. Law firms are increasingly making information available on their Internet sites; CMS Cameron McKenna's "Law Now" site provides details of the latest legal issues in each subject area, news and analysis of developments, with no charge. The LIS input to such information can be recorded but not recharged, so a different ethos has to develop.

Knowledge management, extranets, and the availability of commercial know-how externally are intrinsic to the issue of charging, although these issues will be different within each organisation, and will constantly change. The main objective is to grasp these issues and use them to your advantage. Librarians are professionals too; why should their time not be valued?

Kate Hodgson, Head of Knowledge and Information Management, CMS Cameron McKenna. Tel: +44 (0)20 7367 3000; Fax: +44 (0)20 7367 2000; Email: info@cmck.com; Website: www.cmck.com

8.2 Institute of Advanced Legal Studies, University of London

Introduction

The Institute of Advanced Legal Studies is a postgraduate research institution, which is part of the University of London and has an explicit national and international mission to support and facilitate research in law. The Institute is primarily funded to support academic research and provides facilities for researchers from universities worldwide. However, the Institute has always had strong links with lawyers in other parts of the legal system: the judiciary, practising lawyers and government, and encourages joint research across the different sectors.

The Institute's library is one of the largest legal research libraries in the world and has one of the largest concentrations of law librarians and legal information staff to exploit this material. The library has substantial collections of law from all the jurisdictions of the United Kingdom. It also holds very large collections of foreign, international and comparative law, including unique materials, for example its strong collections of legislation from some Commonwealth countries. The library is the major component of the UK's comparative legal collections; much of the material is unavailable elsewhere in the United Kingdom and is collected by few libraries anywhere.

As a law library, we serve a profession with a strong appreciation of the value of quality information services. We are situated in the heart of a commercial capital, which is one of the world's centres for global legal services. The demand from the various branches of the practising profession for access to the library's collections and its staff's expertise led to the establishment of the library subscription service.

Until 1985, an *ad hoc* document supply service existed in response to demand from the legal profession, but it ran without designated staff, without a proper pricing structure and on a (very) marginal cost recovery basis - essentially the cost of photocopies themselves plus postage. As demand grew, the pressure of this "external" work reduced capacity for the library's primary mission. A new service with dedicated staff and a realistic pricing structure was launched in the late 1980s to serve the legal system and provide a premium service. It has become an important element in servicing the legal system, placing a national collection efficiently at the disposal of lawyers, ranging from the House of Lords to the Incorporated Council of Law Reporting, from the Inns of Court to many of the world's leading law firms.

Services

The subscription service was designed primarily for institutional members, although some individuals have joined. Subscribers gain access to three services:

- personal access to the library, for all members of staff covered by the subscription (usually all members of a law firm); this is a distinct advantage over the alternative of non-transferable daily or longer-term individual membership

- a telephone enquiry service for reference enquiries; this solves problems, offers advice, suggests sources and repairs broken citations

- a document supply service, which is only available to non-academics if they subscribe to the library. The document supply service normally provides a same-day service (frequently within the hour). Subscribers are invoiced monthly in arrears for documents supplied.

Use of the subscription for personal access is still the most popular of these services. Probably this is because of the breadth of access it allows, as subscribers will send in a number of junior members of staff over a year to research particular areas. The advantage for them is that this allows unlimited research use without needing to arrange, and pay for, access on each visit. There is probably a cost saving over individual paid access, certainly true for small firms or sets of chambers that use the library a great deal.

Demand for the document supply service has grown steadily over the past seven or eight years, with only one year in which demand fell. This must reflect partly our position in relation to other sources. We are not the only service for lawyers - for example professional associations also seek to serve lawyers' information needs - but they concentrate on UK law, which is the concern of most of their members. However, the Institute serves a niche market in specialist materials; increasing globalisation in the legal services market has led to the need for those materials. The level of expertise and the speed of response have been vital factors in the success of the services.

The type of material requested and supplied falls very largely into three categories:

- historical material that is not yet easy to access electronically

- comparatively obscure, usually overseas, material for which the Institute is the sole or main UK location

- more mainstream material that is available in electronic form but which a number of lawyers find easier to obtain or prefer to cite in its original printed form (this category is decreasing in proportion to the others).

A substantial proportion of the material is requested for use directly in judicial proceedings. Until recently UK courts would not accept citation of materials produced from electronic sources. This has now changed and may explain the decrease mentioned above. However, some lawyers prefer to provide the court with copies of texts from original printed versions.

The level of demand is difficult to assess in context. The service is able to cover all its costs; it generates a contribution to the overheads of the building and to collection conservation costs every year, which might otherwise fall on the academic budget of the library. Interestingly, the income split between subscriptions and document supply is approximately 60% to 40%. However, the work involved is inversely proportional. The document supply service is permanently staffed, as will be discussed below, whereas the total time taken to administer subscriptions is around two to three days per month for one member of staff. The day-to-day personal use of the library places a demand on the general services, including the general enquiry services, which is more difficult to identify and quantify.

Market

We are lucky in serving a discipline that encompasses solicitors, barristers, in-house law departments in financial services firms, government departments and charities, for whom legal materials are a vital component of their work. All of these join the subscription service. This is partly by virtue of our holdings and partly a result of our location in Bloomsbury, close to the Inns of Court and within reasonable distance of the City of London, where the majority of large law firms are based. Some of our subscribers are based abroad, some in offshore tax havens such as Bermuda, and these join solely for access to the document supply service. Very often, the main attraction seems to be access to the historical material that is out of copyright but not available in electronic form.

At any one time, there are around 200 to 220 subscribers. Many subscribers do not use the document supply service, and it is clear that some London-based subscribers are using the subscription purely for the ease of personal access to the library's collections. The library currently does not identify physical use of the library by individual subscribers; the computer-controlled access system could do this with access cards for each subscribing firm but the emphasis is on ease of access for subscribers. A number of subscribers use the service infrequently and appear to subscribe on the "standing order" principle on the grounds that access to the library may be useful and is certainly less expensive than attempting to create a collection of foreign law in case it may be needed.

The direct customers served by the document supply service are very often the library and information services of the subscribing firms. The subscriber establishes this point of contact as it ensures one cost centre for the firm. Such a channel works well for the Institute's document supply service, partly at least because it ensures that we deal with people who are aware of the nature of legal information and understand what is feasible as a request and what is not. This enables the library to cultivate and maintain close relationships with regular clients. Often fellow law librarians are known personally by staff since the Institute plays a central role in law library training in the United Kingdom. This makes it easy for subscribers to ask questions and for advice on the telephone enquiry service. Visits are arranged for subscribers to view the library and meet enquiry staff, and open evenings arranged so that subscribers and potential subscribers can learn about developments at the Institute. Library staff from subscribing organisations sometimes attend in-house training sessions.

Charges

The charging structure consists of two parts. The initial subscription fee is variable depending on location and size of the subscribing firm. Subscription fees decrease the further a subscriber lives from London, which is designed to reflect the personal use that the subscriber is likely to make of the library.

a) London area (all 020 telephone codes)

	Number of lawyers	Subscription (incl. VAT) (£)
Band 1	1-10	225
Band 2	11-25	335
Band 3	26-50	445
Band 4	51-100	665
Band 5	101-200	1,120
Band 6	201-300	1,860
Band 7	301-400	2,590
Band 8	401-500	3,350
Band 9	501-600	4,090
Band 10	601+	4,820

b) Rest of United Kingdom and EU subscribers not registered for VAT

	Number of lawyers	Subscription (incl. VAT) (£)
Band 1	1-10	160
Band 2	11-25	225
Band 3	26-50	300
Band 4	51-100	445
Band 5	101-200	745
Band 6	201-300	1,240
Band 7	301-400	1,730
Band 8	401-500	2,225
Band 9	501-600	2,730
Band 10	601+	3,200

c) EU subscribers registered for VAT and other overseas subscribers

	Number of lawyers	Subscription (incl. VAT) (£)
Band 1	1-10	135
Band 2	11-25	190
Band 3	26-50	255
Band 4	51-100	380
Band 5	101-200	630
Band 6	201-300	1,055
Band 7	301-400	1,470
Band 8	401-500	1,890
Band 9	501-600	2,320
Band 10	601+	2,725

Document supply charges are calculated on the basis of a handling charge per item plus charges per sheet of photocopy plus delivery, which is charged at cost.

The per item charge consists of the service charge, the photocopying charge, the transmission charge plus VAT where applicable. In January 2003, the transaction charges for each item supplied are as follows:

Service charge: £8.10

Photocopying charge: 22p per sheet

Transmission charge:

Mail

at cost (first class or airmail)

Courier at cost (London only)

Fax (UK & Europe) 85p per sheet

Fax (overseas) £1.85 per sheet

For the document supply service, the charging structure was designed to reflect the actual work involved in providing any one document. It is interesting to see that a similar service at Columbia Law School, United States, uses a very similar charging structure. However, pricing any specific document is complicated and adds a step in proceedings because subscribers are always given an opportunity to review their order once an estimate of costs is made. A more standardised pricing policy might lead to higher turnover at less cost of staff time, although whether it would lead to greater customer satisfaction is debatable.

Administration

Basic administration of the service works as follows.

General admissions office staff deal with all requests for subscriptions and renewal information. Standard format packs have been produced for each stage of the process: request for information, welcome to the service, and subscription renewal. Subscriber details are input and maintained on the customised Access database, which is the principal administrative tool.

Document supply service processing works in two main stages. Each initial request is logged manually on a request form. This has advantages as materials have to be fetched from the stacks and it is simple enough for staff to carry bits of paper around with them.

All fulfilled requests for documents are logged on the customised Access database, which connects documents ordered with subscribers and makes price calculations for each document. The database tracks and monitors requests and automatically generates a number of reports, including monthly statistics and itemised invoices; client references can be attached on request to each record to ease subscribers' own administration.

The monthly financial administration is handled by the Institute, but the main University of London accounts office issues the formal invoices and handles credit management. Manual files of copyright declaration forms are maintained in the section for the statutory period.

The customised Access database was developed for the service and is described in Gee and Whittle (1996). In addition to networked personal computers, the service runs with two photocopiers, which are also shared with library office staff, and two fax machines, one of which is dedicated to the service and one of which is available for all library office staff.

Staffing

The service is run mainly by dedicated staff as a separate unit but housed in the main open-plan staff offices. At any one time, there are up to four members of staff in the document supply service:

- the section manager, who oversees day-to-day

running of the service, staffs the enquiry service one day per week, and undertakes longer-term planning and organisation

- a library assistant to photocopy and despatch materials
- a graduate trainee library assistant, whose job is to retrieve materials and do basic reference work
- one of several experienced, qualified law librarians, drawn from the rest of the library staff on a rota basis, to answer the telephone enquiry line.

General admissions staff also deal with the administration of subscriptions and personal access, and undertake this in conjunction with their work in admitting readers and general library administration. Subscribers on personal visits use all the services, including general enquiry services.

Most experienced staff in the library work in the unit for half a day a week answering enquiries. This is necessary as most subscribers need experienced law librarians to help in tracing documents. Many enquiries do not have a citation and require some research to locate the information that is required. In addition, the two library assistants from the unit spend one afternoon a week working on the main library issue desk. Cross-working helps both library and subscription services staff; everyone seems to enjoy the variety of work. The overlap between "academic library" work and "subscriber" work means there is no neat division of costs to offset against subscription services income, and a programmed budget approach is adopted to analyse costs.

Marketing

At the moment, the service is running at or near capacity. As a result we undertake little marketing to potential new clients. Some promotional activities such as this case study and articles in law library journals, for example Gee (1999), are written on request. We also give an annual reception with tours of the library and presentations to the City Legal Information Group and provide tours on request for actual or potential subscribers. Promotional leaflets are sent out on request and in occasional general mailings; information is also available on our website. Marketing within the subscriber base by personal visits and client consultations has enhanced quality and promoted a close relationship with regular and larger clients.

From experience, the most effective method of marketing for us has been word of mouth. Nonetheless, such marketing as we do is reactive and a fully thought-out marketing strategy needs to be developed.

Successes and problems

The success for this service has been its recognition as a high quality, reliable and friendly service, which is important to the legal system. The service has continued to grow and achieve a satisfactory financial performance, covering all its costs and providing a useful role not available elsewhere. In the initial years before its launch as a unit, the ad hoc service ran on a marginal cost recovery basis - i.e. it was effectively run at a loss, and subsidised by the library's main academic funding. The service now generates enough income to lessen the impact of occasional shocks to the library's main budget, though not to negate these entirely, and to contribute significantly each year to the library's general overheads. Since many of these are fixed, they would otherwise be a charge on the main library budget.

The service is also a major source of job satisfaction for those connected with it. It provides the reward of immediately filling pressing needs, working to strict deadlines, and matching up to the expectations of the most demanding commercial clients. It also becomes a useful training ground for young professionals who want to move on to law librarianship in law firms. In general terms, the culture of quality in the fee-based service percolates through the organisation as a whole and acts as a driver for change.

More immediate issues include the service's financial administration. The Institute is part of the University of London and all financial services come through the University's central accounts office. This has always caused problems with invoicing and payments. It took several years to persuade the central accounting service of the need for itemised invoicing, despite the availability of the information from the Institute's systems. The University is not used to invoicing for services provided and its accounting procedures still need to be faster, more direct and more responsive. It was a long time before credit card payment facilities were authorized, which was particularly important for overseas clients to make payments conveniently. Essentially there is still no commercial imperative for the University authorities to develop in a way that would be easy to achieve in a smaller or more commercial organisation.

A long-term challenge for the service, as for all information services, is the move from paper to electronic publication of material. This puts pressure on the service in two ways. One is that potentially fewer documents will be requested as more material is available online either free or pay-per-view. The other, which we already find, is that the licensing conditions of electronic materials are such that we are unable to supply information from these sources, even when we are the only national source and the subscriber is unlikely to be able to justify a purchase or subscription to the electronic source. Some tentative talks with publishers to help them reach such customers through our services have not yet been successful.

Copyright is a major issue for all document supply services. We may refer subscribers to easily available sources or supply out-of-copyright materials. We also provide documents under the provisions of the Copyright, Designs and Patents Act 1988 and associated copyright regime. However, as a result of the implementation in the United Kingdom, probably by August 2003, of European Directive 2001/29/EC on copyright, we shall no longer be able to supply copies without payment of a copyright fee unless the end user signs a declaration that the copy is required for private study or research that is not for a commercial purpose, or it is for use in judicial proceedings. However, the need for expertise in rare or unusual materials will not disappear and the ability of national collections to contribute to research in other sectors will continue. A mixed mode approach involving rights payments where appropriate may evolve if an efficient system can be made available to ascertain and make the requisite payments. Negotiations are currently being undertaken with the Copyright Licensing Agency for suitable licensing terms. The problem may not be cost, as there is reasonable elasticity in the market, but the need for streamlined and fast systems.

Future directions for the service will be: moving into electronic document delivery; diversifying into other services, such as legal research, charging by the hour; and provision of training courses in legal research skills. These will need new skill sets and equipment and it will be interesting to see whether they can be made as successful as the current service.

Alice Hamilton, former Legal Information Services Manager, Institute of Advanced Legal Studies. For the subscription services tel: +44 (0)20 7862 5800; Fax: +44 (0)20 7862 5850; Email: ials@sas.ac.uk; Website: ials.sas.ac.uk

8.3 MONINFO, Monash University Library, Victoria, Australia

Monash University is a global university with eight campuses, including one in Malaysia and one in South Africa, and centres at King's College London and in Prato, Italy. Monash is Australia's largest university, energetic and dynamic, and committed to leading the way in higher education and research.

Rationale for establishing MONINFO

MONINFO is a fee-based initiative of Monash University Library which was established in 1990 with a charter to:

- release reference staff from external inquiries without any conflict of priority so they could focus on the University's primary clientele, the students and staff

- satisfy a perceived need to provide an information service to business and industry using the expertise of Monash University Library staff

- build partnerships with business and industry thus promoting the Library and University to the broader community

- provide an alternative source of funding for the Library in an era of ever diminishing budgets; the current theme of self-reliance embedded in the University plan puts greater emphasis on income generation and entrepreneurial activities.

Staffing

We are a small, dedicated unit of three staff: a manager, an information specialist, and an office co-ordinator who handles document delivery, membership and invoicing. Like any small team, when the pressure is on we all pitch in and do what ever has to be done to meet deadlines, even if it is folding letters and sealing envelopes.

Ostensibly MONINFO can employ the expertise of specialist subject librarians to assist with research although it rarely happens as their work pressures are onerous and our clients' deadlines tight. However, we can tap into these librarians' expertise and discuss appropriate resources for unusual requests. In the past, we have employed consultants to assist if we are inundated with research requests, but to maximise profits we attempt to keep all jobs in-house. We employ a consultant one day a week to manage a small company library and to author its website. We are masterful jugglers, consummate conjurers, mind contortionists and deadline tightrope walkers; in fact Cirque du Soleil might be grateful to have our dexterity!

Who are our clients?

We have no stereotypical clients; clients' backgrounds are just as diverse as their information requests. Individuals, small businesses with just a few employees, government departments and large multinational corporations employing thousands all share the same need for information. They represent most business sectors; high-tech information-intensive industries and pharmaceutical companies outnumber other client groups. Quite a number of companies have been loyal clients for a decade and we are their cost-effective surrogate library with a skilled research assistant always on tap.

We conduct patent and citation searches for academics at Monash University and research for other commercial business units within the University. Overseas clients seeking Australian-related material gravitate to our site. The Law Library collection attracts international clients, particularly for the world-renowned Australia Pacific law collections of primary and secondary materials.

Suite of services

We are a one-stop information provider and have the expertise to tackle most projects.

Our services are pay-as-you-go with no up-front subscription costs. Document delivery and information research are our core businesses:

Document delivery Clients may place requests by letter, phone, fax, email or via a form on our website. We source documents from the extensive collections of our campus libraries, and globally through a network of copyright cleared suppliers. Our service is personalised, customer friendly and efficient. Many companies have established MONINFO as their preferred supplier. The legal profession relies on our super-fast track, one-hour service providing cases for barristers in court. We add value by verifying incomplete or incorrect citations.

Information research Clients may apply by fax, email, phone or the search form on our website. As we seldom see our clients in person, the telephone interview is crucial in probing the search topic, and we may contact clients for further clarification if we need to limit or expand the parameters of the topic. Once a deadline is agreed, and a quote accepted, then the search may proceed. Each search is allocated a job number and entered into an Access database with client, topic, searcher, deadline date and budget recorded. Each element of data provides valuable information for management and analysis. Most searches are completed within three to five working days but major investigations may take up to six weeks to carry out and some urgent searches are required within 24 hours. On one occasion a magazine rang in desperation requesting a diagram of the brain indicating the section affected by migraine. Within half an hour we had located a suitable diagram and sent it by courier to the magazine's office to make the publication deadline.

We rarely say no; however, there was a job we declined from a man in China with thousands of unprocessed bloodied sheep fleeces, which he wanted to import into Australia. He was referred to Austrade and Customs.

We are infrequently daunted and will undertake research on any topic, some of which are quite bizarre. Some are nebulous; once we were asked to divine females' perceptions of where germs lurk in the home. Several months later we recognized our contribution to the project in a television advertisement launching a new range of antibacterial products depicting a mother and housewife protecting her family against the ravages of germs.

Our challenges have included anthropological kinship data on remote tribes in Irian Jaya, best practice in discharging patients from emergency hospital departments, medico-legal cases, bioavailability and degradation products of particular drugs, portable loos with a privacy screen designed for women, and business competitive intelligence.

An update service is offered to clients who need to monitor product, company or industry trends regularly.

Other services include:

- conducting primary market research - designing and administering telephone interviews and presenting the results in a spreadsheet
- ordering books, journals, standards and patents for companies
- developing and maintaining web pages
- managing specialised libraries
- assisting with speeches, including compilation of background biographical data
- citation verification of bibliographies before a paper is submitted for publication

- Internet training seminars tailored to an organisation's needs and skill levels

- workshops on how to develop complex search strategies

- compiling webliographies for particular industries

- promoting and administering library membership for external borrowers in the categories - corporate, individual, school and alumni

- publications - Asian Source Books were compiled by the Asian Studies Research Library staff and published by MONINFO; an Australian Business Source Book is scheduled for publication in 2003

- conducting information audits for companies seeking ISO accreditation

- research for patent attorneys providing accession dates of when an item would have first been available for public consultation in Australia

- cataloguing specialist collections by contracting expert cataloguers from Technical Services to MONINFO for off-site work

- a translation service, which taps into the pool of linguistic expertise with native speakers of all Asian languages who work in the Library.

Promotional activities

A mix of promotional strategies has been tried over the years: some were innovative, a few were debacles, and others gave us more bang than we could have possibly hoped for from our marketing buck.

In this industry, we are always on the hustle to expand our business with every encounter viewed as a chance to meet a prospective punter. Business cards are secreted in our briefcases and cocktail bags, ready for every occasion. Aeroplanes are a particularly good venue with a captive market! We have tried or considered the following promotional activities:

- *Internal promotion.* This is often neglected and the adage that everyone is a potential client is worth remembering. Library staff on reference desks are pivotal points of referral. MONINFO has given lunchtime talks to Library staff titled "Living on the Edge", or "The Importance of Not Being Overly Earnest!" We role-play some interactions with demanding clients, starring a bombastic barrister garbed in wig and gown, a debonair Dr Doolittle dangling a stethoscope and a blood pressure monitor, and a dapper businessman garbling management speak.

- *Air-time.* With a degree of scepticism, we accepted a special deal: a radio station was offering airtime supposedly targeting our client group. It was a complete flop, none of our staff ever heard the ad and, worse still, it did not generate a single lead.

- *Television shows.* Targeted at small business, television shows would be a good forum for an interview on how MONINFO can improve the bottom line. We are still waiting for the call!

- *Website.* Our website will be one of the key platforms of promotion.

- *Articles.* In professional journals, articles usually attract an initial flurry of interest.

- *Presentations.* Presentations to professional organisations, including special interest library groups, have proved valuable in the past.

- *Targeted mail-outs.* If targeted, mail-outs to national industry groups can be effective.

- *Exhibitions.* Exhibitions provide an opportunity to showcase our services and to promote them to other traders as well as to the public. Business cards are collected in a bowl and lucky prizes are drawn. None of the winners has been exactly jubilant. Somehow a free search does not have quite the same appeal as a swim with the dolphins!

- *Bulletins.* Bulletins have been issued irregularly to stay in touch with clients and prospects and to inform them of new services.

- *Visits.* Visits to existing clients are a cost-effective means of promoting the entire range of our services.

- *Pro-active promotion.* Examples of pro-active promotion are sending a letter congratulating a company on winning a business award and offering a free half-hour's consultancy, or a journal article on a competitor; and sending an email to a radio station with the cost of a kidney in India, after an on-air discussion of harvesting body parts for commercial gain.

- *Links.* There are links from significant and influential government and commercial websites to our site.

- *Brochures.* Brochures were an integral part of our promotion for many years but are now considered passé by the marketing gurus. They are expensive to produce and we rely increasingly on other avenues of advertising. We may revisit the brochure debate in 2003.

- *Directory entries.* Entries in Australian and international commercial directories can bring in new business.

- *Business breakfasts.* We have found these an excellent forum for networking.
- *An advisory group.* The MONINFO Advisory Group comprised businessmen and women from different industries to recommend strategies to increase our profile. It was abandoned in favour of focus group meetings.

Resources

MONINFO subscribes to the main Australian and international vendors of databases. Print is not dead and the resources of the Monash University Library, with over 2.6 million items, are invaluable assets. We have a competitive edge through our ability to connect business with academic research.

Confidentiality

Confidentiality is one of our core values and it is always guaranteed. Some clients require us to sign a confidentiality clause, particularly for classified government projects. At times our confidentiality has been truly tested but even under threat of torture our lips were sealed.

Disintermediation and the Internet

Dreadful term predicting dire results. As more clients turned to the Internet as the first port of call our business took a nosedive. However, it wasn't long before the novelty wore off and clients returned to MONINFO, frustrated by fruitless and time-wasting searching. We advised them to be wary of information obtained solely from the Internet, as the authority, currency and accuracy of the material needed close scrutiny. A more serious warning was that they were missing valuable information that we could retrieve from well-organised commercial databases.

Competitors or allies?

We track our competitors for changes to their schedule of fees or service streams.

In the 12 years MONINFO has been operating, many information brokers have gone under, including several at academic institutions. We have an excellent working relationship with a number of key players whom we regard as allies. The more players there are in the marketplace the easier it is to create awareness of the value of our superb information product.

Marketing and promotion

The University has introduced a standard for visual identity, which governs the appropriate use of the elements that comprise the Monash identity, including the University name, logo, colours and shield. Sadly, MONINFO has lost its distinctive logo, in gold and blue, which appeared on our entire stationery and website, but we could reap greater leverage from the more prominent University branding.

Every accolade is kept on file for a multitude of purposes, including promotion. Brickbats are resolved immediately to the client's satisfaction. Suspicious bells ring if a client complains twice, in which case we negotiate an outcome that is equitable to both parties. There is no third complaint!

Money matters

MONINFO is a self-funding unit annually returning a profit to the Library. Managing MONINFO is like running a small business with a constant eye on the bottom line and exercising financial diligence. The University has selected SAP as its financial accounting system. We use SAP to raise and track invoices and identify potentially delinquent clients who may default on payment.

We accept payment by credit card, cheque, cash, deposit account, and we will be offering an e-commerce facility in the not too distant future. We always provide a quote first, based on an estimation of our time and all other direct costs, including database access, fax, courier, and so on. A quick dip into the appropriate databases gives us an indication of the number of hits we can expect to retrieve. An hourly consultancy is charged with an additional surcharge for fast track research. Many repeat clients dispense with the quote and nominate their own budget. Over the years experience has taught that it is better to quote a range of charges for complex searches and an all-inclusive project charge for really large jobs.

Undeniably external factors have impacted dramatically on business confidence; since 11 September 2001 many businesses are floundering and the consequent job losses are undermining the economy. Some government information has been withdrawn from the Internet. The future is uncertain but information brokers will have a crucial role to play.

How'd you like to have fun, fun, fun?

Work should be fun. Without humour to dispel the pressure cooker atmosphere the team would be burnt out and quite deranged. So:

- Aim to exceed your clients' expectations.

- Make your encounters with prospective punters professional and positive.

- Dare to be different with presentations and you will be remembered.

- Be passionate about your work. If you stop being inquisitive and only do it for the money, it is time to move on. As cybersleuths, we love the thrill of the chase and, with adrenaline pumping, we dissipate the data smog to reveal the kernel of knowledge that will delight the client.

Finally, check us out at www.lib.monash.edu.au/moninfo

Margaret Pratt, Manager, MONINFO.
Tel: +61 (0)3 9905 2690; fax: +61 (0)3 9905 1424;
email: moninfo@lib.monash.edu.au;
Website: www.lib.monash.edu.au/moninfo

8.4 Business Research and Information Service (BRIS) of the Institute of Financial Services

Introduction

The Institute of Financial Services (*ifs*) is the official brand of the Chartered Institute of Bankers, a professional body that conducts examinations and awards qualifications to those in the financial services sector. It has always provided a range of services to its membership, including a library, which was established along with the Institute itself in 1879. Until recently, what perhaps was less well known to those working outside the banking profession was the additional range of information services being developed and offered more widely. How did this come about and what is now on offer?

In 1951 the Library moved to a new London location at 10 Lombard Street and remained there until 1996. The Library provided traditional lending services to its members and dealt with enquiries mostly via telephone and fax. Although the way in which information was provided moved on with the advent of enhanced technology, it was from 1996 onwards that key changes in information provision took place, with the move to new London premises at 90 Bishopsgate. It was also during this period that the Institute introduced a new brand name, the Institute of Financial Services (*ifs*), for its range of products and services, while retaining the title Chartered Institute of Bankers for the assessing and awarding body.

The Business Research and Information Service is established

The new glass-fronted premises, based in the heart of the City, and conveniently at a traffic-stop location, attracted interest from the wider business community, such as lawyers and management consultants. In 1997, in response to the resultant requests and enquiries from this wider community, the Business Research and Information Service (BRIS) was established. The aim of BRIS is to extend information services to business and financial institutions outside the Institute's traditional membership base and to be the commercial arm of the former library, now the Institute's Information Service. The new service was advertised in the Institute's magazines and prospective city clients were invited to an open evening, which proved a great success, attracting a number of potential clients from various sectors.

BRIS is housed in a separate office with dedicated, specially trained staff. It has its own brand identity, a separate brochure and also has pages on the *ifs* Information Service website at www.ifsis.org.uk, which provides details of the range of services on offer.

Pricing structures

When setting out as a fee-based service, BRIS had to make decisions about pricing structures: whether to have a pay-as-you-go time usage charge, a flat fee or a subscription arrangement. It was decided to introduce several different levels of subscription to suit different-sized companies with different information needs and these were discussed with corporate customers. BRIS now has a number of corporate subscribers at different levels and from various business sectors, but also handles one-off research enquiries with the fee individually negotiated and based on a cost-plus basis - i.e. staff time, plus costs of use of sources and services, such as document production and supply, including photocopying and courier transfer. These individual enquiries are charged at £50 + VAT per half-hour.

At the time of writing there are five levels of subscription for businesses:

- GOLD, the premium service currently costing £2,500 + VAT per annum

- SILVER

- BRONZE - currently the most popular subscription scheme

- SMALL BUSINESS

- SOLE TRADER, at present £250 + VAT per annum - a service aimed at consultants and individuals using the library for business purposes.

The different subscription schemes offer various amounts of free research, a number of entrance cards for users to have access to the information service and use of sources, book loans, document delivery and other services, according to the level chosen by the subscriber. Details of the different subscriptions are given below.

The GOLD subscription provides:

- entrance to the library and access to its resources for up to 8 cardholders

- 10 hours of free research (worth £1,000 + VAT) with any additional research at only £30 + VAT per half-hour

- free reference enquiries

- up to 30 book loans at one time
- free delivery of information by fax or post
- free access to Internet resources in the library
- articles and document delivery available at a nominal charge
- 5% discount on most books in the Financial World Bookshop
- free subscription to the Institute's journal "Financial World".
- The annual cost is £2,500 + VAT.

The SILVER subscription provides:

- entrance to the library and access to its resources for up to 6 cardholders
- 5 hours of free research (worth £500 + VAT) with any additional research at only £30 + VAT per half-hour
- free reference enquiries
- up to 18 book loans at one time
- free delivery of information by fax or post
- free access to Internet resources in the library
- articles and document delivery available at a nominal charge
- 5% discount on most books in the Financial World Bookshop
- free subscription to the Institute's journal "Financial World".
- The annual cost is £1,000 + VAT.

The BRONZE subscription provides the following benefits:

- entrance to the library and access to its resources for up to 4 cardholders

- 3 hours of free research (worth £300 + VAT) with any additional research at only £30 + VAT per half-hour
- free reference enquiries
- up to 12 book loans at one time
- free delivery of information by fax or post
- free access to Internet resources in the library
- articles and document delivery available at a nominal charge
- 5% discount on most of the books in the Financial World Bookshop
- free subscription to the Institute's journal "Financial World".
- The annual cost is £600 + VAT.

The SMALL BUSINESS subscription is designed specifically for small businesses with a turnover of less than £1 million per annum who may not have access to a library or information centre. It offers:

- entrance to the library and access to its resources for 2 cardholders
- 2 hours of free research (worth £200 + VAT) with any additional research at only £30 + VAT per half-hour
- free reference enquiries
- up to 12 book loans at one time
- free delivery of information by fax or post
- free access to Internet resources in the library
- articles and document delivery available at a nominal charge
- free subscription to the Institute's journal "Financial World".

• The annual cost is £400 + VAT.

The SOLE TRADER subscription offers:

- entrance to the library and access to its facilities for the individual cardholder
- 1.5 hours of free research (worth £150 + VAT) with additional research at only £30 + VAT per half-hour
- free reference enquiries
- up to 6 book loans at a time
- free delivery of information by fax or post
- free access to Internet resources in the library
- articles and document delivery available at a nominal charge.
- The annual cost is £250 + VAT.

As well as the above, all subscriptions also offer access to EBSCO Business Source Elite, an online full text database of articles.

BRIS can also provide other services, such as the details of banking expert witnesses. Unsuccessful searches - those yielding little or no information for whatever reason - may carry a charge for research time. Before work is undertaken clients are advised on possible costs and time involved for any more substantial research.

Staffing

Although ultimately the aim of BRIS is to generate income, its minimum requirement is to recover all the costs involved in the provision of information. While BRIS has a separate identity, branding and brochure, it is seen as an integral part of the information service with the sharing of resources, including staff knowledge and skills. Information sources purchased may be used both by the general information service and BRIS, or items may be bought by BRIS for specific purposes or projects.

All the information staff work closely to ensure maximum effectiveness for both services. This also provides flexibility in terms of staff cover. A good example of joint working by staff of the Information Service and BRIS is the publication of the *City & Financial Services Contact Directory 2002*, which lists contact details for major financial institutions in the United Kingdom such as banks, building societies, stockbrokers and others. Whilst this is a publication from the information service as a whole, the project was managed by the BRIS manager.

Adaptability and commercial sense are key requirements when working in a business environment, so when staff are recruited considerable emphasis is placed on such attributes. As well as good research skills, an understanding of the business environment and the expectations of those working within it are essential. Staff must also feel comfortable with the practice of charging for information, know how to explain it and be able to negotiate and communicate with clients. If you are offering a service that depends on its success as a fee-based entity you will want clients to keep coming back and to spread the word, so marketing and presentation skills also play a key role. Staff training for BRIS is developed individually as required; it is important that staff have an agreed co-ordinated approach to service provision, and seek and share information on new sources and techniques that might enhance the service. Feedback from clients also contributes to the process of continual improvement and, now that the BRIS has been up and running for a while, more formal monitoring is planned.

Sarah Watts, Manager, BRIS at the Institute of Financial Services

Tel: +44 (0)20 7444 7123/7132; Fax: +44 (0)20 7626 8138; Email: bris@ifslearning.com; Website: www.ifsis.org.uk

Chapter 9

References and further reading

Abell, Angela et al. (1995) *Critical Success Factors for Fee-based Information Services*. (British Library R & D Report, no.6172) Hatfield: University of Hertfordshire Press. c. 67 pages.

Advertising Standards Authority (2003) *British Codes of Advertising and Sales Promotion*. 11th ed. London: ASA. c. 50 pages. Due for publication on 4 March 2003. Can be downloaded from the ASA website (www.asa.org.uk) or the Committee on Advertising Practice website (www.cap.org.uk) without charge. Email alerting service for developments if you register an interest profile.

Broadhurst, Dominic and Julie Brown eds (1999) *Where to Buy Business Information 1999*. East Grinstead: Bowker-Saur, Headland Press imprint. 177 pages.

Brophy, Peter and Kate Coulling (1996) *Quality Management for Information and Library Managers*. Aldershot: Aslib Gower. c. 200 pages. Guide to quality management theory and practice in relation to information services. Includes consideration of tools such as service standards and performance indicators, and chapters on the customer perspective, TQM, the mission of the library, effectiveness and systematic performance measurement, and implementing quality management.

City and Financial Services Contact Directory 2002 (2001) Canterbury: Financial World Publishing (the publishing arm of the Chartered Institute of Bankers). Includes CD-ROM.

Coffman, Steve (1999) "Special considerations for fee-based services in public libraries", in Ward, Suzanne M. et al. (1999) *Information Delivery in the 21st Century: Proceedings of the Fourth International Conference on Fee-based Information Services in Libraries*. New York: Haworth, pp. 13-28. Offers insights into establishing and maintaining fee-based services and defining the dividing point between free and fee services based on his experience as director of a fee-based service, FYI, at Los Angeles Public Library.

Coote, Helen and Bridget Batchelor (1997) *How to Market Your Library Service Effectively*. 2nd ed. (Aslib Know How Guide) London: Aslib. c. 60 pages. A concise introduction, which covers market research, the key elements of a marketing strategy, positioning in the marketplace, and the four Ps: product, price, plan and promotion.

Cornish, Graham (2001) *Copyright: Interpreting the Law for Libraries, Archives, and Information Services*. Revised 3rd ed. London: Library Association. 210 pages.

Corrall, Sheila (2000) *Strategic Management of Information Services: a Planning Handbook*. London: Aslib. 364 pages. A thorough treatment of management and planning issues. See particularly chapter 5, "Money matters", pp. 156-206. Includes annotated guides to further reading for each topic.

Egholm, Charlotte and Henrik Jochumsen (2000) "Perspectives concerning user fees in public libraries", *Library Management* 21 (6), pp. 298-306.

European Code of Practice for Information Brokers. Luxembourg: EUSIDIC. 20 pages. The Code is promulgated by EUSIDIC (European Association of Information Services), EIIA (European Information Industry Association) and EIRENE (European Information

Researchers Network) and is available from EUSIDIC, PO Box 1416, L-1014, Luxembourg. Tel: +352 250 750 220; Fax: +352 250 750 222.

European Union (2001) Directive 2001/29/EC of 22 May 2001 on the harmonisation of certain aspects of copyright and related rights in the information society. *Official Journal of the European Communities*, 22 June 2001, L167, pp. 10-19.

"Fee-based information services" (1999) *Law Librarian* 27 (2). A special issue of about 70 pages containing a survey of services in the United Kingdom related to business and law and about 18 brief articles on different services including Information for Business at Westminster Central Reference Library, the British Library, Lloyd's, Columbia Law School in New York, London Business School, Manchester Business School, the Institute of Directors, and Birmingham public libraries, among others.

"Fees for library service: current practice and future policy" (1986) *Collection Building* 8 (1), Special issue.

Fong, Yem S. (1999) "Pricing and costing in fee-based information services", in Ward, Suzanne M. et al. (1999) *Information Delivery in the 21st Century: Proceedings of the Fourth International Conference on Fee-based Information Services in Libraries.* New York: Haworth, pp. 63-73. Reviews cost accounting methodology and pricing models from a US perspective.

Gee, David (1999) "Charging for information services at the Institute of Advanced Legal Studies Library", *Law Librarian* 30 (3), 169-72. Type and range of commercial information services offered by IALS Library, development of a charging structure.

Gee, David and Steven Whittle (1996) "Introducing an automated management system for the document supply service at the IALS", *Law Librarian* 27 (2), 111-14. The procurement and operation of a customised database system to manage contacts, subscriptions, and track and invoice enquiries.

Information Commissioner (2001) *Data Protection Act 1998: Legal Guidance.* Wilmslow, Cheshire: The Commissioner. 104 pages. This is available in print or for download from the Commissioner's website at www.dataprotection.gov.uk.

Lyon, E. et al. (1998) *Impact of Devolved Budgeting on Library and Information Services in Universities in the UK.* (British Library Research and Innovation Centre Report, 138). London: BLRIC. A report on research into the nature of devolved budgeting introduced in UK universities, including implementations of service level agreements and internal charging structures, and the effect on the overall performance of the library and information services. Contains considerations and conclusions relevant to all sectors.

MacKintosh, Pamela J. (1999) "Writing an effective business plan for fee-based services", in Ward, Suzanne M. et al. (1999) *Information Delivery in the 21st Century: Proceedings of the Fourth International Conference on Fee-based Information Services in Libraries.* New York: Haworth, pp. 47-61. The basics of writing a business plan drawn from traditional business literature in the US adapted to information services with extensive references.

McKay, Duncan (2003) *Effective Financial Planning for Library and Information Services.* 2nd ed. (Aslib Know How Guide) London: Europa Publications. 100 pages. A concise guide to financial planning with an example budget.

Mowat, Mary (1998) *Legal Liability for Information Provision.* (Aslib Know How Guide) London: Aslib. c. 60 pages. A concise introduction to the legal issues, in terms of contractual obligations, negligence and duty of care, arising in the provision of information, both for a fee and free service, and management practices to minimise risk.

Norman, Sandy (1999) *Copyright in Industrial and Commercial Libraries.* 4th ed. London: Library Association. 80 pages.

Oppenheim, Charles. "LISLEX: legal issues of concern to the library and information sector", *Journal of Information Science.* A regular column for current awareness published since about 1994 in this journal, which appears six times per year.

Pantry, S. and P. Griffiths (2001) *The Complete Guide to Preparing and Implementing Service Level Agreements.* 2nd ed. London: Library Association. 208 pages. An introductory textbook, which covers service descriptions, quality issues and charging.

Pedley, Paul (2000) *Copyright for Library and Information Service Professionals.* 2nd ed. London: Aslib. c. 120 pages. A practical guide for information professionals, with advice and reference to the relevant legislation and regulatory materials covering printed and electronic materials and uses.

Roberts, Stephen A. (1998) *Financial and Cost Management for Libraries and Information Services.* 2nd ed. London: Bowker-Saur. 406 pages. A comprehensive work on cost measurement and accounting in the context of strategic planning and management. Includes extensive citation to the literature on the subject both in relation to information services and more generally.

Scammell, Alison ed. (2001) *Handbook of Information Management.* 8th ed. London: Aslib. c. 500 pages. Comprehensive work including chapters on information audit, performance measurement, financial planning, project management, marketing, copyright, data protection and legal liability.

Tilson, Y. (1994) "Income generation and pricing in libraries", *Library Management*, 15 (2) 1994, pp. 5-17. Based on research by questionnaire and interview of academic, public and special libraries in London. Covers pricing models, policies and attitudes regarding cost recovery and income generation and where to draw the line between free services and fee-based services.

Wall, Raymond A. (2000) *Copyright Made Easier*. 3rd ed. London: Aslib. 548 pages. Written in collaboration with Sandy Norman, Paul Pedley and Frank Harris. A comprehensive treatment of the subject with practical advice and discussion of rights of ownership and permissions, and coverage of a broad range of other aspects of intellectual property in relation to information including database rights, moral rights, design rights and performance rights.

Ward, Suzanne M. (2000) "The client satisfaction survey as a tool for evaluating library fee-based information services", *Journal of Interlibrary Loan, Document Delivery and Information Supply* 10 (3), pp. 63-76.

Ward, Suzanne M. et al. (1999) *Information Delivery in the 21st Century: Proceedings of the Fourth International Conference on Fee-based Information Services in Libraries.* New York: Haworth. Published separately and as *Journal of Interlibrary Loan, Document Delivery and Information Supply* 10 (1) 1999. Contains a range of articles with a US perspective including contributions to the "fee or free" debate, considerations for fee-based information services in public libraries and in academic libraries, writing a business plan, pricing and costing, copyright considerations with reference to US law and a positive view of the future for information professionals in the fee-based environment. Some articles from this publication are also cited individually in this list.

Webb, Sylvia P. (1996) *Creating an Information Service*. 3rd ed. London: Aslib. 150   pages. A practical guide to all aspects of setting up an information service, with examples, checklists and further reading.

White, Brenda (1992) *Maintaining the Balance: External Activities in Academic Libraries* (BLRD Research Report no.100) London: British Library Research and Development Department. About 120 pages. Contains several detailed case studies.

Will, Colin (2000) "Information is not free", *Impact* 3 (8), pp. 119-20.

Winterton, Jules and Elizabeth M. Moys eds (1997) *Information Sources in Law*. 2nd ed. London: Bowker-Saur. 673 pages.

Appendix: List of organisations

Advertising Standards Authority
2 Torrington Place
London WC1E 7HW
Tel: +44 (0)20 7580 5555
Fax: +44 (0)20 7631 3051
Email: inquiries@asa.org.uk
Website: www.asa.org.uk

Business Research and Information Service (BRIS)
90 Bishopsgate
London EC2N 4DQ
Tel: +44 (0)20 7444 7123/7132
Fax: +44 (0)20 7626 8138
Email: bris@ifslearning.com
Website: www.ifsis.org.uk

Chartered Institute of Library and Information Professionals
(formed in April 2002 by the merger of the Library Association and the Institute of Information Scientists)
7 Ridgmount Street
London WC1E 7AE
Tel: +44 (0)20 7255 0500
Fax: +44 (0)20 7255 0501
Email: info@cilip.org.uk
Website: www.cilip.org.uk

Committee of Advertising Practice
2 Torrington Place
London WC1E 7HW
Tel: +44 (0)20 7828 4224
Fax: +44 (0)20 7637 5970
Email: enquiries@cap.org.uk
Website: www.cap.org.uk

CMS Cameron McKenna
Mitre House
160 Aldersgate Street
London EC1A 4DD
Tel: +44 (0)20 7367 3000
Fax: +44 (0)20 7367 2000
Email: info@cmck.com
Website: www.cmck.com

Copyright Licensing Agency
90 Tottenham Court Road
London W1T 4LP
Tel: +44 (0)20 7631 5555
Fax: +44 (0)20 7631 5500
Email: cla@cla.co.uk
Website: www.cla.co.uk

Direct Marketing Association (UK) Ltd
DMA House
70 Margaret Street
London W1W 8SF
Tel: +44 (0)20 7291 3300
Fax: +44 (0)20 7323 4165
Email: dma@dma.org.uk
Website: www.dma.org.uk

EIRENE: European Information Researchers Network
Sissel Hafstad, President
NHH Library
Helleveien 30
N-5035 Bergen-Sandviken
Norway
Tel: +47 5595 94 04
Fax: +47 5595 94 44
Email: sissel.hafstad@nhh.no
Web: www.eirene.com

Information Commissioner
Wycliffe House
Water Lane
Wilmslow
Cheshire SK9 5AF
Tel: +44 (0)1625 545 745
Fax: +44 (0)1625 524 510
Email: data@dataprotection.gov.uk
Website: www.dataprotection.gov.uk

Institute of Advanced Legal Studies
University of London
17 Russell Square
London WC1B 5DR
Tel: +44 (0)20 7862 5800
Fax: +44 (0)20 7862 5850
Email: ials@sas.ac.uk
Website: ials.sas.ac.uk

Institute of Directors
116 Pall Mall
London SW1Y 5ED
Tel: +44 (0)20 7839 1233
Fax: +44 (0)20 7930 1949
Email: enquiries@iod.com
Website: www.iod.com

Institute of Financial Services *see also* BRIS
IFS House
4-9 Burgate Lane
Canterbury
Kent CT1 2XJ
Tel: +44 (0)1227 762600
Fax: +44 (0)1227 763788
Email: customerservices@ifslearning.com
Website: www.ifslearning.com

Institute of Information Scientists <u>see</u> Chartered Institute of Library and Information Professionals

Library Association <u>see</u> Chartered Institute of Library and Information Professionals

London Business School Business Information Service
Regent's Park
London NW1 4SA
Tel: +44 (0)20 7723 3404
Fax: +44 (0)20 7706 1897
Email: infoserve@london.edu
Website: www.bestofbiz.com

MONINFO
Matheson Library
Box 4
Monash University
Clayton 3800
Victoria
Australia
Tel: +61 (0)3 9905 2690
Fax: +61 (0)3 9905 1424
Email: moninfo@lib.monash.edu.au
Website: www.lib.monash.edu.au/moninfo/

Newspaper Licensing Agency
7-9 Church Road
Wellington Gate
Tunbridge Wells TN1 1NL
Tel: +44 (0)1892 525273
Fax: +44 (0)1892 525275
Email: copy@nla.co.uk
Website: www.nla.co.uk

The Patent Office
Harmsworth House
13-15 Bouverie Street
London EC4Y 8DP
Tel: 0845 9 500505 (UK callers)
Tel: +44 (0)1633 813930 (international callers)
Fax: +44 (0)1633 813600
Email: enquiries@patent.gov.uk
Website: www.patent.gov.uk

Index

Italic letters after page numbers indicate these types of content:

a = address
b = bibliographic reference
c = case study
f = figure

O
objectives 36, 75
operational considerations 35-8
Oppenheim, Charles 42, 111*b*
overheads 28-9, 30, 69, 79, 86

P
Pantry, S 40, 48, 111*b*
Patent Office 43, 119*a*
pay-as-you-go 39, 91
payment 39-40, 50-1, 87, 97-8
Pedley, Paul 42, 111*b*
performance measures 39, 64
performance targets, staff 64
personal information, data protection 41, 59
planning 5-8, 27-44
potential, assessment 35-8
Pratt, Margaret 99
presentations, oral 61, 94
press monitoring 63-4
press releases 60
pricing 33-5
    BRIS 100-4
    see also charging
pro-active promotion 95
procedures 45-54
procedures manual 46-7, 48, 49, 50, 51-2, 54
professional ethics 41
professional indemnity insurance 40
profit 29-30, 33-4, 97
progress reviews 12
project leader 10, 12
project team meetings 12
promotion *see* marketing and promotion
publications, for marketing 57-8
publicity *see* marketing and promotion

T - #0144 - 270225 - C0 - 198/129/8 - PB - 9780851424750 - Gloss Lamination